Goldwin Smith

Loyalty, Aristocracy and Jingoism

Three Lectures Delivered before the Young Men's Liberal Club, Toronto

Goldwin Smith

Loyalty, Aristocracy and Jingoism
Three Lectures Delivered before the Young Men's Liberal Club, Toronto

ISBN/EAN: 9783337002848

Printed in Europe, USA, Canada, Australia, Japan

Cover: Foto ©Suzi / pixelio.de

More available books at **www.hansebooks.com**

LOYALTY, ARISTOCRACY

AND

JINGOISM.

Three Lectures

Delivered before the Young Men's Liberal Club, Toronto,

BY

GOLDWIN SMITH, D.C.L.

Toronto:
HUNTER, ROSE & COMPANY,
AND
WILLIAMSON & CO.
1891.

The following Lectures were delivered before the Young Men's Liberal Club, of Toronto, in February, May and November, 1891. It is not necessary to say anything by way of preface, except that the position of the Lecturer and his audience was not aggressive but defensive, the Lectures having been called forth by the vehement and systematic attacks of the Conservatives on the character of the Liberals for loyalty and patriotism at the time of the last general election.

G. S.

Toronto, November 12th, 1891.

LOYALTY.

YOU have done me the honour, Gentlemen of the Liberal Club, to desire that I should read you an address on the subject of "Loyalty." I gladly respond to your request. But you will allow me to address you on this occasion as liberal-minded men, not as Liberals in the party sense of the term. I have been asked, as I am with you in this struggle, why I do not join your party ? I reply that I am with you and with anyone in a struggle such as that on which you are now entering against Commercial Monopoly and Government by Corruption, and hope with other citizens to do my best in the day of battle ; but when I am invited to join a party my answer must be that I have always steadfastly set my face towards national government, and that I and others, if there are any, who think as I do, are more likely to be useful by being true to our own principle, and saying what there is to be said for it, than by compromising it in order to take a more active part in politics. Then I am not sure about my qualification for

*Delivered before the Young Men's Liberal Club, Toronto, February 2nd, 1891.

admission. A Liberal in England I was held to be, and
even a thorough-going Liberal, though I always had a
rooted abhorrence of violence and revolution. But I am
not sure that I should pass muster with your organization. Perhaps as an Englishman I am biassed, but so it
is that I believe the integrity of the United Kingdom to
be essential to its greatness, and its greatness to be essential to the balance and the progress of European civilization. Therefore I could never take part in helping the
enemies of British unity for the purpose of conciliating
the Irish vote. I pleaded, like John Bright, for justice
to Ireland in days when the Irish vote was not so much
regarded,* but I am afraid I should be a bad hand at conciliating the Irish vote now. I think with sorrow of the
thraldom into which the Anglo-Saxon communities have
fallen. Again, while I am absolutely free from the
slightest prejudice against the Roman Catholics, among
whom have been some of my dearest friends, it would be
impossible for an old European Liberal, a friend of Mazzini and Garibaldi, to enter into an alliance with Jesuits
and Papal Zouaves, or to refrain from opposing priestly
usurpation. I am conscious, too, that I am a Liberal of
the Old School, one of those who wish Government to
mind its own business, who desire that at last man
should have a chance of self-development, and who are
no more inclined to submit to the tyranny of majorities
calling themselves the State than to the tyranny of

---

*See note at the end of this Lecture.

kings. Perhaps the best reason of all is that at my time
of life it is too late to put on new harness, and a man can
only go on his own way supporting what he thinks right
and opposing what he thinks wrong. With those who
are fighting against Monopoly and Corruption no good
citizen can hesitate to take part.

But to the question. It is not wonderful that you
wish just now to get all the information you can about
loyalty. The air is full of loud professions of it, and still
louder denunciations of disloyalty. The suspicion of
disloyalty evidently entails serious consequences, extending in certain contingencies to being sabred by some
loyal warrior on the street. What is, perhaps, of more
practical importance is that the cry, by its effect on
nervous persons, is likely to prevent the fair considera-
tion of questions vital to the welfare of our people.

There certainly is something peculiar about this virtue. There is a species of it, at all events, which very
happily coincides with self-interest. The loyal are
sometimes like the Puritan Saints, who deemed it their
religious duty to inherit the earth. Conquerors and
oppressors, for instance, always call submission loyalty
and patriotism treason. Again, loyalty seems, unlike
other virtues, to find a home in breasts in which no
other virtue can dwell. No men ever were louder or
probably more sincere in their professions of it than were

Scroggs and Jeffreys at the time when they were
judicially murdering Russell and Sidney or going on the
Bloody Assize. The carpet-baggers who governed and
swindled the South after the Civil War, in like manner,
overflowed with it, and whenever they had been detected in some gross act of corruption the defence was
that they were always "truly loil." On the other
hand, in breasts where the other virtues, political as
well as social, do undeniably dwell in full measure,
we find this virtue strangely absent. In the British
Empire loyalty seems to have the peculiarity of being
eminently colonial. It is like the reverence for the
Papacy, the intensity of which was always found to
vary in direct proportion to the distance from Rome.
At the Plimsoll banquet the other night, after we had
listened to the usual declamations on this theme, a
speaker remarked that Mr. Plimsoll might know he was
not in England, but in Canada, when he heard so much
about loyalty, of which nobody boasted in England.
This remark was true as well as neat. In England you
never hear a word said on the subject. Everybody
takes it for granted that you are not in a plot to over-
turn the dynasty. Suppose a lady were to go about in
society assuring everybody that her hair and teeth were
her own, that her complexion was not paint, and that
the lines of her figure were those laid down by nature,
would she not be apt to create the suspicion which she
was so anxious to avert?

What is the original signification of the word?
Loyauté means respect for law and fidelity to obligation.
Shakespeare uses it for fidelity to the marriage vow, to
filial duty, to friendship, as well as for fidelity to the
king. Milton makes Comus offer the lady the shelter of
a "loyal" cottage, that is, a cottage true to the law of
hospitality. The term especially denoted fidelity to
those feudal obligations which were the organic law of
the time. Those obligations were reciprocal; it was not
only the vassal that owed duty to the lord; the lord
also owed duty to the vassal. If the lord did not per-
form his duty, the vassal renounced his allegiance by a
regular form, called defiance. De Montfort and the
patriot barons thus formally renounced their allegiance
to Henry III. Divine Right was not the creed of those
days, nor was there any blind and spaniel-like devotion
to the person of the king. The feudalists were rough,
but they were not fools; if they had been they could not
have founded European society and the British Constitution. Edward I, the greatest of all feudal monarchs,
was no fetich, but a noble man living in free and frank
intercourse with his peers, foremost in battle and ad-
venture, claiming loyalty by a right truly divine. It is
not till we come to the Tudor despotism that the
fetichism begins. Before Henry VIII., a bloated monster
of selfishness and vice, steeped in uxoricide and judicial
murder, his slaves grovel in the dust. They compare
him to the sun in its glory and almost to God. Adula-

tion well-nigh equally extravagant is paid to his daughter, though in this case the baseness is redeemed by the generous illusion which saw the nation imperson- ated in its queen. Shakespeare, however, you will see, though thoroughly monarchical, is never slavish. But it is with the Stuarts that Divine Right appears as the courtiers' creed, and that loyalty arrogates the character of a distinct virtue. Bishops tell James I. when he in- sults the Puritans that he speaks by the inspiration of God, and divines preach before Charles I. the doctrine that there can be no such thing as justice between the king and the subject any more than between God and the creature. Now it is that the hearts of all who support Stuart despotism, in the words of the Cavalier song, are " crowned with loyal fires." We respect the tradition of the Cavaliers as we respect any tradition of gallantry and misfortune. Some of those men really sacrificed estate and life for what they sincerely believed to be the right, though there was also a large element of what Carlyle calls "truculent flunkeyism." But nobody in England would think of bowing his head to the descendants of the Cavaliers or letting them settle the destinies of the nation. The grass has grown over the graves of Edge- hill and Naseby, as it must grow at last over all graves. The other day, when on a visit to England, I found my- self in the house of a friend who represented one of the Cavalier families. The relics of Charles the First's stand- ard-bearer at Edgehill hung on the walls, but the family

were leading Liberals. However, it was under the
Restoration, and especially at the evil close of Charles
the Second's reign, that the Loyalists became a regular
party, supporting royal usurpation and judicial murder,
and being well paid for their devotion. North, himself
a strong Tory, describes that party as the men that went
about drinking and huzzaing. One of the loudest of
them was Chief Justice Scroggs, of whom North says,
" that he was of a mean extract, having been a butcher's
son, who wrought himself into business in the law," that
he was " a great voluptuary, being a companion of the
high Court rakes," and "had a true libertine principle."
" Scroggs," North tells us, " was preferred for professing
loyalty, but Oates, coming forward with a swinging
popularity, he took in and ranted on that side most im-
petuously." The same men, under the same romantic
designation, combined to support the tyranny of James
II, and to help him in cutting the throat of national
liberty. But when James the II. laid his hand upon the
rich possessions of the Church, the other side of loyalism
was seen. We can understand the King's surprise and
partly sympathize with his disgust. However, loyalism
soon recovered itself, and after calling in William of
Orange to deliver it, it began to show its fidelity to
principle by plotting against his Government and life.
Presently it proceeded to signalize itself by betraying the
the nation at Utrecht, and afterwards by a series of half-
tipsy intrigues and pot-valiant swaggerings in the in-

terest of the " King over the Water." A more despicable
party than the Jacobites, who seemed to themselves and
in a certain sense were, the very pink of loyalty, never
appeared on the scene of history. It is needless to say
how loyalism repaired its golden fires under George III.,
how passionate was its devotion to the person of that
excellent monarch, especially when he was out of his
mind, and what services it rendered to the country by
bringing on the American war and vetoing Catholic
Emancipation. Places, pensions, bishoprics, deaneries,
and sinecures without number, were its reward.

In Canada loyalty was at its zenith under the " Family
Compact." But again it showed its peculiar character as
a virtue. So long as the Crown was on its side, gave it
all the patronage and emoluments, and protected it
against reform, it was passionately devoted to the Crown
and the mother country. But when with the growth of
the Reform movement in England the Crown changed
its policy, a change came over the spirit of Colonial loyalism also. When two Family Compact officials were
dismissed for opposing the Liberal policy of the Government, Loyalist organs began to proclaim that their
attachment to the Empire had received a fatal shock
and that they would have to turn their eyes elsewhere.
Afterwards we know what an exhibition of loyalty
ensued upon the passage of the Rebellion Losses bill.
The principle of the Loyalists upon that occasion, it

must be owned, was severely tried; but it did not prove
equal to the trial. Flinging rotten eggs and stones at
the Governor-General was a singular display of devotion
to the Crown. We need not insinuate that on that
account loyalty was insincere. The African believes in
his idol though he whips it for not giving him what he
wants.

In the days of old the idol of loyalty was, at all
events, a substance, not a shadow, as it still is in countries really under monarchical government, and in which
the people look up, like children, for the maintenance of
order and almost for their daily bread to their paternal
king. But how is it with us? Sunday after Sunday
we solemnly pray to God that Her Majesty and Her
Majesty's representative may be enabled to govern us
well. Let Her Majesty or Her Majesty's representative
presume to do a single act against the wishes of the
Tory Prime Minister; let either of them veto a single job
or bribe, and we know what would be the result. Yet
we profess to believe that God is not to be mocked.
This professed devotion to an empty name is, however,
not without its substantial use. By loud protestations
of loyalty to the Crown, which he knows will never cost
him anything, a man absolves himself from loyalty to the
commonwealth. He feels himself perfectly at liberty to
cabal and conspire as much as he pleases against the
public good in his own interest, or in that of some ex-

clusive order or sectional combination, because he is loyal
to a Crown divested of all its power, and to the name of a
connection with the mother country which he has practically reduced to a mere shadow. I do not mean to
speak disrespectfully of any feeling which is genuine,
however out of date, but there are not a few cases in
which loyalty to the Crown is a fine name for disloyalty
to the country, and loyalty to British connection is a
fine name for disloyalty to Canada.

The loyalty cry is now being raised, in default of any
economical argument, to deter the country from accept-
ing the benefits of Reciprocity and to scare it into
acquiescence in a policy of which commercial atrophy and
the exodus are the visible and inevitable results. Here
we see with what curious exactness a Loyalist's virtue
follows the lines of his own interest through all their
twistings and windings. To exclude British goods by
protective duties is perfectly loyal. It is perfectly loyal
to wage what in fact is a tariff war against the mother
country. But to discriminate against the mother country
is disloyal in the highest degree. The very thought of it
is enough to almost throw a loyal man into convulsions.
Yet discrimination would have no disloyal object. It
would be not against England in particular but against
all countries alike. It would evince no change of feeling
towards the mother country, or towards the political connection. It would not take a penny from the revenue of

the Crown or a particle from its power or dignity. It would hardly take away anything from the commercial wealth of the British people. The enhanced value of their Canadian investments which would result from free trade would probably make up to them for the loss which a few exporting houses would sustain. But the same measure would expose the protected manufacturers of Canada to Continental competition. Therefore he who proposes it is a traitor.

The commercial unity of the Empire is at an end. It was formally declared to be at an end when an Australian colony claimed the right to lay protective duties on British goods, and the question having been considered by the Home Government was decided in favour of the claim. Great Britain has withdrawn all commercial privileges from the colonies, and by the same act she has conceded to them the liberty of doing the best they can commercially for themselves, each according to the circumstances of its own case. The commercial circumstances of Canada are those of a country placed alongside a great neighbour who is under the protective system, and whose policy it is impossible for her in regulating her own to ignore, as it is to ignore the physical features of her continent. The commercial unity of the Empire having been, I repeat, dissolved by the act of the mother country herself, which deprived the colonies of their privileges, there can be nothing disloyal in recognizing the necessities of our own case. Offer us free trade with the whole world, the mother country included, and there are some of us who will gladly accept it. Will the loyal men of the Red Parlour do the same?

We are disloyal, it is said, because we propose to enter into a tariff arrangement with the United States, and by entering into a tariff arrangement with the United States, we should compromise the fiscal independence of the country. Of course you cannot make a treaty without surrendering to that extent, and so long as the treaty lasts, your independence of action. But if the treaty is fair, where is the dishonour? Was there any dishonour in the Elgin Treaty? Was there any dishonour in the commercial treaty made by England with France? It is idle to think that in commercial matters we can be entirely independent of the United States. We must be beholden to them for our principal winter-ports. We must trust to their comity for the transmission of our goods in bond. Our railway system is bound up with theirs. What we call our great national road, the road which was to be the pledge of our eternal separation from them, not only has branches running into their territory, but actually passes with its trunk line through the State of Maine. If there is any disloyalty in this matter it would appear to be in maintaining a fiscal policy which is constantly driving the flower of our population over the line, and saves Canada from annexation by annexing the Canadians.

Does anyone want to be told what is really disloyal ? It is disloyal to assemble the representatives of a particular commercial interest before the elections and virtually sell to them the policy of the country. It is disloyal to seek by corrupt means the support of particular nationalities, churches, political orders, or sectional interests of any kind, against the broad interest of the community. It is disloyal to sap the independence of provinces and reduce them to servile pensioners on the Central Government by systematically bribing them with "better terms" and federal grants. It is disloyal to use the appointments to a branch of the national legislature as inducements to partisans to spend money in elections. It is disloyal to use public works, which ought to be undertaken only for the general good, for the purpose of bribing particular constituencies. It is disloyal to make concessions to public contractors which are to be repaid by contributions to an election fund. It is disloyal to corrupt the public press, and thus to poison the wells of public instruction and public sentiment. It is disloyal to tamper with the article of the Constitution respecting the time of general elections by thimblerigging dissolutions brought on to snap a national verdict. It is disloyal to vitiate the national verdict by gerrymandering. It is disloyal to surrender the national veto on provincial legislation, the very palladium of nationality, out of fear of the Jesuit vote. All corruption is disloyalty. · All sectionalism is disloyalty. All but pure, straightforward and honourable conduct in the management of public affairs is disloyalty. If it is not disloyalty to a Crown on a cushion, it is disloyalty to the Commonwealth.

"Loyalty" still has a meaning though the feudal relation between lord and vassal has passed away. It means thorough-going and self-sacrificing devotion to a principle, a cause or the community. All that is contrary to such devotion or tends to its disparagement, is still disloyal.

The question of our political relations is not now before us. We are dealing with the commercial question alone. But suppose the political question were before us, would there be any disloyalty in dealing with it frankly and honestly? I say frankly and honestly. There is disloyalty in any sort of intrigue. But who has intrigued? According to the Government organs the country is a nest of conspirators. Everybody who goes to Washington goes for the purpose of conspiracy, as though real conspirators would not have the sense to keep their names out of the hotel book. I have myself been charged in the Government organ with going to Washington to sell the country. I go to Washington every Spring on my way with my wife to a Southern watering-place, and at no other time, mainly for the purpose of seeing personal friends, the chief of whom was the late Mr. Bancroft. I have been charged by the same

organ with being a party to bringing American money
into the country for the purpose of influencing the elections, the evidence being that my friend, Mr. Hallam, to
whom I never said a syllable on the subject of political relations, had proposed to raise a fund for the diffu-
sion of knowledge about the tariff question.* Treason is
a great crime. If anybody has been guilty of it let him be
brought to justice. But it is time that people should know
that to charge your fellow-citizens, men in as good standing as yourself, with treason and with trying to sell the
country, without any proof of the fact, is a social offence.
He who, for the purpose of his own ambition or gain,
falsely divides the community on such lines, is himself
guilty of the most pernicious treason.

There has just been a meeting of Imperial Federationists, of whose aspiration I desire to speak with all respect. The object of Imperial Federationists is to make
a great change in our political relations. They seek to
reverse the process of decentralization which, apparently,
in obedience to the dictate of nature, has been going on
for so many years, to take from Canada a part of her
self-government, and to place her again under the authority of a central power. They fancy, indeed, that
they can have an Imperial Federation without detracting
from colonial self-government. But how could this be

---

*It has since appeared that the very persons who brought this charge themselves did
not scruple to take toll of an American firm for a political purpose.

when each of the colonies would be subject certainly to
military assessments, and probably to fiscal control; for
it is hardly possible to imagine a federation with a multi-
plicity of tariffs, some of them hostile to others, as those
of protectionist colonies now are to the mother country?
What the plan of the Imperial Federationists is remains
a mystery. They tell us not to ask them for a cut-and-
dried scheme. We do not ask for a scheme either cut or
dried, but only for one that shall be intelligible and a
possible subject of discussion. Readjustment of postage-
rates is not confederation. However, it lies not in their
mouths to say that a proposal of change must be disloyal.
If they are at liberty to advocate centralization, "Canada
First" was equally at liberty to advocate independence.
"Canada First," in its day, was denounced as disloyal. I
well recollect when you were told that to speak of Canada as a nation was treason. We have now got beyond
that point, I suppose, since adherence to the National
Policy is now the height of loyalty. If there is any
question of loyalty in the matter it might be thought
that they were the most loyal who desired for their country a higher position than that of perpetual dependence.
Whether their aspirations were feasible is another question. They hardly took into account the French difficulty, nor did they or perhaps anybody at that time
distinctly see what effect the enormous extension of disjointed territory toward the West would have on the
geographical unity of the nation. But their aspiration

was high; they were responding in fact to the appeal which the authors of Confederation themselves had made to the heart of the country, and never was the name of loyalty more traduced than when they were called disloyal.

There are men living, high in public life and in the Conservative ranks, who signed a manifesto in favour, I do not say of Annexation, which is a false and hateful term, but of political union with the United States. Nothing is more irrational or ungenerous than to taunt people with opinions which they once honestly held and have since not less honestly renounced. It is not for any such purpose that I refer to the Montreal manifesto. But such a manifesto could not have been signed by such men if the question were not one which might be entertained without disloyalty, provided always that those who entertain it remain firm, pending its solution, in their dutiful allegiance to their own country. For my own part, being not a politician, but a student, and restrained by no exigencies of statecraft, I never conceal my opinion. I have always deplored the schism which divided our race a century ago. I hold that there was wrong on both sides, and not less on the side of the American Revolutionists than on that of the British Government. I hope and steadfastly believe that some day the schism will be healed, that there will be a moral reunion, which alone is possible, of the American colonies

of Great Britain with their mother country, and a com-
plete reunion, with the hearty sanction of the mother
country, of the whole race upon this continent. Great
Britain will in time see that she has no real interest
here but amity and trade. The unity of the race, and
the immense advantages of a settlement which would
shut out war from this continent and make it an economical whole, will prevail, I feel convinced, in the end
over evil memories and the efforts of those who cherish
them. That the consummation will come in my time is
unlikely, though a Government of monopoly and corruption is driving it on apace. At all events, I have no
more personal interest in it than in any astronomical
event. Nor would I wish to see it hastened by any
means which would impair its perfect spontaneity. On
the other hand, nobody who believes in ultimate union
can wish to see the earnings of the people wasted in
desperate efforts to perpetuate separation. A hundred
millions of public money or money's worth, at least, have
been spent on this great national road by which the triumph of the Separatist policy was to be secured forever.
Not a Yankee was to have a cent in the enterprise or to
have anything to do with it, and the road was to run
entirely over our own territory, not touching the accursed
Yankee soil. The road has been built partly with Yankee money; it had for some time an eminent Yankee
politician for its vice-president; it has now a Yankee
for its president; it runs through the Yankee State of

Maine, and connects our system with the Yankee system at more points than one. It is, in fact, half a Yankee road. So much for the wisdom and hopefulness of a fight against Nature.

Whether Commercial Union would accelerate political union or retard it, who can say? The Elgin Treaty manifestly put off political union by removing discontent. But railway union and social union and the fusion of the populations by the exodus all manifestly tend to political union, and who thinks it disloyal to contribute to these? If a man makes himself prominent in cultivating loyal antipathy to Americans, you are as likely as not to find that he is in the service of an American railroad company and helping, honourably enough, to send Canadians to the States. The other day I was myself reviled in the most unmeasured language for my supposed American proclivities. Soon afterwards I heard that my assailant had accepted a call as a minister to the other side of the line.

On this continent, not in Europe; in the New World, not in the Old; the lot of Canada and of Canadians is cast. This fixes our general destiny, whatever special arrangements of a political kind the future may have in store. This sets the mark of our aspirations and traces the line of our public duty. This determines for us what is genuine loyalty. That course of action which leads to the happy development of man on our own continent is for us loyal. To say that loyalty consists in keeping this community always in dependence on a community three thousand miles off and condemning it to be without a life of its own, is to set loyalty at fatal odds not only with nature but with genuine sentiment. Nature assigns us not only the more practicable but the nobler part.

It is irrational to rail against British aristocracy. British aristocracy is an historical institution; it had its day of usefulness in its own country; and perhaps in its own country, if it faces the crisis gallantly, it may do some good still. But it can do no good here. It can breed and does breed nothing here but false ambition, flunkeyism, title-hunting, and sycophantic Resolutions. It draws away the hearts of wealthy and ambitious Canadians from their own country to Downing Street and Mayfair. Let it retire to its own land. To sacrifice Canada to its policy and make her a perpetual engine in its hands for preventing the triumph of democracy on this continent is to put her to service which loyalty to her and to humanity as well as good sense abhors. Let British aristocracy, I repeat, do the best it can and live as long as it can in Great Britain : it has no business here. It is said, I believe truly, though it was not reported at the time, that when the Mulock Resolution was put one very eminent member of the Opposition uttered some manly words and went out of the House.

He carried true loyalty with him and left something
that was not loyal or true behind. Let British aristocracy withdraw with grace from a world for which it has
done nothing and which has never belonged to it. The
Governor-Generalship surely would not be a great loss
to it. How can any man of mark or spirit wish to play
the part of a figure-head, or, worse still, by the exercise
of his mock prerogative to help in loading the dice for a
gambling politician ?

There might be danger and there might be disloyalty
in touching this question if there were on the part of
Americans any disposition to aggression. But there is
none. If the Americans meditated annexation by force,
why did they not attack us when they had a vast and
victorious army ? If they meditate annexation by pressure, why do they allow us bonding privileges and the
use of their winter ports ? The McKinley Bill was eager-
ly hailed by Separatists here as an act of American hos-
tility. Its object was simply to rivet and extend protection, at the same time catching the farmer's vote, for
which politicians fish there with the same bait with
which Sir John Macdonald fishes here. Of course as
there are paper tigers on our side of the line, there are
tail-twisters on the other side. One of the most valiant
of them, in the person of Senator Ingalls, has just bitten
the dust. The tail-twisters have as much influence there
as the paper tigers have here, and no more. These sus-

picions when unjustified are undignified. They expose
us to ridicule, while they prevent us from seeing in its
true light and settling wisely the great question of our
own future.

Those who say that the country is suffering from a bad
fiscal policy and from the corruption of government are
branded as disloyal. They are charged with decrying
Canada by telling this unpleasant truth. Truth, pleasant
or unpleasant, can never be disloyal. But let the accus-
ers look back to their own record before 1878, when the
opposite party was in power. What pictures of national
distress and ruin were then painted! What pessimism
was uttered and penned! What jeremiads rung in our
ears! Soup kitchens, some thought, were opened not so
much for the relief of distress as to present in the most
vivid and harrowing manner the state to which Liberal
policy had reduced the people. Is it the rising flood of
prosperity that is sending so many Canadians over the
line? It was disloyal to say that railway monopoly was
keeping back the North-west. What do they say about
that now?

Is it loyal to turn our Public Schools into seedplots of
international enmity by implanting hatred of the Americans in the breasts of children? The Public Schools are
maintained by all for the benefit of all, and it is an
abuse of trust to use them for party purposes. Nor does
it seem very chivalrous to be inveigling children instead

of appealing to men. Celebrations of victories gained in byegone quarrels over people who are now your friends are perhaps not the sort of things to which the bravest are the most prone. Wellington and the men who had fought with him at Waterloo used to dine together on that day. This was very well, especially as those victorious veterans did not crow or bluster. But it forms no precedent for boastful demonstrations by us, who did not fight at Queenston Heights or Lundy's Lane. And when this war spirit is got up, whom are we to fight? The one million of Canadians and their half-million of children now settled on the other side of the line? All the British immigrants who have been pouring into the United States during the last generation? Literally, when we take away from the population of Canada the French and other nationalities, there would be as many men of British blood on the enemy's side as on ours. "Bombard New York!" said a Canadian of my acquaintance; "why, my four sons live there!"

Is it loyal to threaten us with settling questions on horseback, in other words, with military coercion? The English people would not endure such threats from the commanders of the army which won the Alma and Inkerman. I heard one of these tirades read out at a Commercial Union meeting by a tall farmer, who when he had done said, "Now we want no nonsense"—whereat a number of other tall farmers with deep voices cried,

"Hear! hear!" There is force enough, let us hope, in the country to vindicate its own freedom of deliberation and its power of self-disposal. The only effect of menaces such as are sometimes heard will be to make our people more deaf than ever to the appeals of British Imperialists who exhort us to maintain a standing army as a safeguard for our independence. Our independence is safe enough from any hostile aggression, and our liberty is safer in our own hands than in those of warriors who propose to decide political questions for us on horseback.

Loyalists appeal to the memories of those who fought and fell at Queenston Heights and Lundy's Lane. We also appeal to those memories. Honour to the brave who gave their lives for Canada! As they did their duty to their country then by defending her against unjust invasion, they would now, if they were alive, be doing their duty to her by helping to rescue her from monopoly and corruption. Honour, once more, to the truly brave! Let us build their monuments by all means. We are all as ready as any Loyalist to contribute, if only we may be allowed, to make the memorial, like the joint monument to Wolfe and Montcalm at Quebec, a noble and chivalrous tribute to heroism, not an ignoble record of a bygone feud, and to grave on it words expressive not of perpetual enmity, but of the reconciliation of our race.

Let us be true to the country, keep her interest above all other interests, personal, partisan, or sectional, in our hearts ; be ready to make all sacrifices to it which a reasonable patriotism demands ; be straightforward and aboveboard in all our dealings with public questions, and never, out of fear of unpopularity or abuse, shrink from the honest expression of opinion and the courageous advocacy of whatever we conscientiously believe to be good for the community. So long as we do this, depend upon it, we are loyal.

NOTE.

There appeared some time ago in the New York *Tribune* an extremely personal criticism, extending over nearly three columns, on my life and character, by Mr. E. L. Godkin, the New York journalist, an Irishman and Home Ruler. The ostensible occasion was the sequel of a journalistic passage-of-arms. The article was inaccurate in its representations, depicting me among other things as a man who had been all his life restlessly dabbling in political journalism, the truth being that I had no connection, except of the most casual kind, with any political journal between 1858, when I retired from the staff of the *Saturday Review* on my appointment to the professorship of Modern History at Oxford, and 1872, when at the instance of friends I became, for a short time, a contributor to the Toronto *Nation*. I was also represented as having proposed the suspension of Trial by Jury in Ireland, when, in fact, I had done nothing of the kind. I, however, allowed the attack to pass without notice, not being inclined to engage in an autobiographical discussion in the New York Press, while I felt sure that American readers would have too much sense to accept any man's portrait as painted by a manifest enemy. The main charge, however, was that of "diabolical" behaviour and language with reference to the Irish question, notably in relation to a lecture delivered by me at Brighton, England, as Mr. Godkin supposes in 1881, in opposition to Mr. Gladstone's Irish Land Bill, but really delivered in 1882, after the passage of that Bill, of which, as well as of Disestablishment, I spoke in the lecture with gratitude, though I could not help feeling misgiving. The spirit of this "diabolical" production will be seen from the concluding paragraph, in which it is summed up :—

"Be not weary of well-doing. Remember, in half a century of "popular government, how much has been effected, what a mountain

" of abuses, restrictions, monopolies, wrongs, and absurdities has been
" cleared away. In face of what difficulties has this been achieved !
" what prophecies of ruin have all along been uttered by reaction or
" timidity, and how one after another have those prophecies been
" belied ! In the case of England and Scotland, the fruits of a Liberal
" policy are visible in a wealthier, a happier, a better, a more united,
" and a more loyal people. In the case of Ireland they are not so clearly
" visible ; yet they are there. The Ireland of 1882, though not what
" we should wish her to be, is a very different Ireland from that of the
" last century, or of the first quarter of the present. Catholic exclu-
" sion, the penal code, the State Church of the minority are gone ; in
" their place reign elective government, religious liberty, equality
" before the law. A system of public education, founded on perfect
" toleration of all creeds, and inferior perhaps to none in excellence,
" has been established. The Land Law has been reformed, and again
" reformed on principles of exceptional liberality to the tenant.
" Wealth has increased, notwithstanding all the hindrances put in the
" way of its growth by turbulence ; the deposits both in the savings'
" banks and in the ordinary banks bear witness to the fact. Pauper-
" ism has greatly declined. Outrage, on the average, has declined also,
" though we happen just now to be in a crisis of it. Under the happy
" influence of equal justice, religious rancour has notably abated ; the
" change has been most remarkable in this respect since I first saw
" Ireland. Influential classes, which injustice in former days put on
" the side of revolution, are now at heart ranged on the side of order
" and the Union, though social terrorism may prevent them from
" giving it their open support. The garrison of Ascendancy, political,
" ecclesiastical, and territorial, has step by step been disbanded ; an
" operation fraught with danger, because those who are deprived of
" privilege are always prone in their wrath to swell the ranks of dis-
" affection, which yet has been accomplished with success. If the
" results of political, religious, and educational reform seem disappoint-
" ing, it is, as I have said before, because the main question is not the
" franchise, or the Church, or the public school, but the land. With
" this question a Liberal Parliament and a Liberal Government are
" now struggling ; while its inherent difficulties are increased by Tory
" reaction on the one side and by Fenian revolution on the other. Of
" all the tasks imposed by the accumulated errors and wrongs of ages,
" this was the most arduous and the most perilous. Yet hope begins
" to dawn upon the effort. Only let the nation stand firmly against

"Tory and Fenian alike*, and against both united, if they mean to
"conspire, in support of the leaders whom it has chosen, and to whose
"hands it has committed this momentous work.   If separation even
"now were to take place, what has been done would not have been in
"vain.   Ireland would go forth an honour to England, not a scandal
"and a reproach, as she would have been if their connection had been
"severed sixty years ago.   If any one doubts it, I challenge him once
"more to compare the state of Ireland with that of any other Roman
"Catholic country in the world.   But of separation let there be no
"thought ; none at least till Parliament has done its utmost with the
"Land question and failed.   Let us hope, as it is reasonable to hope,
"that where so much has been accomplished, the last and crowning
"enterprise will not miscarry.   ,Settle the Land question, and that
"which alone lends strength to political discontent, to conspiracy, to
"disunion, will be gone.   Passion will not subside in an hour, but it
"will subside, and good feeling will take its place.   The day may
"come when there will be no more talk of England and Scotland
"governing Ireland well or ill, because Ireland, in partnership with
"England and Scotland, will be governing herself, and contributing
"her share to the common greatness and the common progress ; when
"the Union will be ratified not only by necessity, but by free con-
"viction and good will ; when the march of wealth and prosperity will
"be no more arrested by discord, but the resources of the Island will
"be developed in peace, and the villas of opulence perhaps will stud
"the lovely shores, where now the assassin prowls and property cannot
"sleep secure ; when the long series of Liberal triumphs will be
"crowned by the sight of an Ireland no longer distracted, disaffected
"and reproachful, no longer brooding over the wrongs and sufferings
"of the past, but resting peacefully, happily. and in unforced union at
"her consort's side.   The life of a nation is long, and though by us
"this consummation may not be witnessed, it may be witnessed by
"our children."

In the body of the work I said :—

"I am anti-Imperialist to the core, and firmly convinced that political unions, not dictated by nature, are condemned by true wisdom, and
can be sources of nothing but discord, unhappiness and weakness.   To
et Ireland go in peace after what has happened would be difficult.   It

---

*This had reference to the relations of a section of the Tory party, under Lord
Randolph Churchill, with the Parnellites.

is one thing never to have been married, another to be divorced. For some time, at all events, the relation would be one not of mere independence, but of enmity. Still, if we do not feel sure that it is good for Ireland to be in the Union, and if she wants to be released, in Heaven's name let her go. I will drop the first condition, and say, even though you do feel sure that it is good for Ireland to be in the Union, if the deliberate wish of the whole, or anything like the whole, of her people is separation, separated let her be."

Mr. Godkin asserted that my language in private was even more diabolical than my language in public. Whether my language in public was diabolical has been seen. How Mr. Godkin knows what was my language in private, I am not aware; but I am not conscious of having done more than express the natural feelings of humanity at atrocities, such as the Phœnix murder and a number of others, which every Irishman in whose breast party passion has not extinguished hatred of murder must equally reprobate and deplore as disgraceful to his country.

My little work on " Irish History and Irish Character," published in 1862, was, I believe, about the first attempt to present the case in favour of justice to the Irish peasantry, with reference to the Land question, in a historical form. It received the warmest commendations of men whose position as Irish patriots could not be questioned. The progress of historical research has since detracted from any value it may have as a history; but the opinions expressed in it remain on all material points unchanged. It concludes with an argument in favour of the maintenance of the Union on much the same grounds on which I advocate the maintenance of the Union now. This is the answer to the charge of apostacy, whether it comes from Mr. Frederic Harrison or from any other quarter. The allegiance of Liberal Unionists was to their principles not to the person of a leader, and in refusing to turn round with a leader they have not changed their principles.

ARISTOCRACY.[*]

RISTOCRACY, on which I am briefly to address you this evening, has once more become a subject of practical interest for us here. Knighthoods we have long been enjoying; but knighthoods, not being hereditary though they are feudal, are hardly aristocratic. Now, baronetcies are again being created, and colonial peerages are being conferred. We are called upon again to consider whether social distinction on the hereditary principle can be usefully implanted here.

Louis XIV., as we all know, tried to create an aristocracy in Quebec. Though his absolute monarchy had been founded on the ruin of feudalism, and he had emasculated the feudal nobility by turning them from local lords into the courtiers of Versailles, Louis was socially an aristocrat to the core. He withheld an archbishopric from Bossuet because the greatest man of the French Church was a commoner, while a nobleman of scandalous life was archbishop of Paris. But not even the fiat of the

*Delivered before the Young Men's Liberal Club, Toronto, May 11th, 1891. The Lecture has been partly revised with reference to subsequent developments, especially the creation of Colonial Peerages.

great king could make the plant of Privilege take root
in the soil destined for Equality. A single barony remains the lonely monument of his design. Even this for
some time fell into abeyance or ceased to be legally
recognized, and only by family effort was it restored. For
the rest, Louis seems to have succeeded merely in calling
into existence a certain amount of ragged pride, insolence
and idleness, probably not unlike the noblesse of "white
trash," which used to loaf about the Slave States, giving
itself high airs because it did not work.

Pitt, the Tory Minister of Great Britain, projected for
Canada a hereditary House of Lords, by him and his
party deemed the first of political blessings. Fox warned
him that the field was unsuitable and that he would fail.
Fail the great Tory Minister did, more completely even
than the great French King. A House of Lords would
plainly be a house of shreds and patches without hereditary estates: a peer who had to peddle small wares for
his living in the morning, could not assume much dignity
or authority in the evening, even if you set him in a
hall of state; and hereditary estates in a colony, as Fox
foresaw, there could not be. No political peerage ever
came into existence. We have, it is true, a faint shadow
of the House of Lords in our nominee Senate, with its
gilded chairs. This is the nearest approach made to the
fulfilment of Pitt's idea. A branch of the legislature
nominated by a Minister of the Crown out of his personal
adherents and the contributors to his party fund, has, at

all events, little enough to do with popular institutions.
Combined with a power of dissolution, which makes the
tenure of the other branch of the legislature dependent
on the Minister's will, and with a power practically almost unlimited of expending public money for local ob-
jects, it is likely to make our Parliamentary system what
all the Governors-General tell us, and we boast that it is,
a pre-eminently pure and perfect expression of the con-
victions and wishes of the people!

To found a social aristocracy, a feeble attempt was
made by the creation of baronetcies, those curious demi-
peerages invented by James I. for the replenishment of his
exhausted exchequer, and sold by him in market overt
at the price of £1,000 apiece. In England a baronetcy is
often the half-way house on the road to a peerage. But
like a peerage it requires hereditary wealth to support
its respectability. It was perhaps for this reason that so
few Colonial baronetcies were conferred. The practice
seemed to have been given up. A baronet out at elbows
would be almost as shocking to humanity as a peer.
Now, however, the practice is revived, apparently by the
Tory reaction which has set in against the growing
tendency of the Colonies to independence, and we are
once more invited to judge in notable instances how close
is the relation between hereditary title and public virtue.

Not only Colonial baronetcies but Colonial peerages are
being created manifestly in pursuance of the same policy

of reaction. The Colonial peer, however, is to take his seat not at Ottawa, as Pitt's peers had they come into existence would have done, but at Westminster, where we may safely say they will be of all lords the lordliest and the least Colonial. This is the mildest of all the forms of Imperial Federation. Wealth is the one indispensable qualification for hereditary honour, and a fresh stimulus will no doubt be given by this policy to the accumulation of Colonial fortunes, perhaps not always by the noblest means. To suppose that a millionaire translated to Westminster and Mayfair can be accepted as a representative by Canada or allowed to exercise an influence over our affairs is absurd. If any authority is conceded by the British legislature to Colonial peers on that assumption, the British legislature will be utterly misled. The transfer of great masses of wealth produced by Colonial industry from the Colony to London and the propagation among Colonists of a false aim for their ambition, are the benefits which the Colonies are likely to derive from the creation of a Colonial peerage.

The nearest approaches to social aristocracy which this continent has seen probably are the Dutch landowners of New York and the Planters of Virginia. An old Dutch lady was told that it was intended to alter the name of the Dutch Reformed Church and call it simply the Reformed Church, to make it more comprehensive.

" I don't want it made comprehensive ! " she replied, " it
is the Church of the old Dutch families of this State."
The claims of the Slaveowners of Virginia to figure as
representatives of exiled cavaliers has, like the Norman
pedigrees of the British peerage been a good deal shaken
by genealogical criticism : but supposing them to have
been only Slaveowners, they were not less worthy of
worship than the horde of robbers which came with
William the Conqueror to England, and from which aristocracy is so anxious to trace descent.

Let us say at once that in discussing aristocracy we
are not discussing the use of titles. To titles there can
be no reasonable objection so long as they go with a public trust or denote service done to the State. Government by force having here no place, reverence for lawful
authority is the rock on which we must build; and till
our natures become far more ethereal than they are now,
some outward symbols will be necessary to sustain our
reverence. We do not lower ourselves by giving the
title of honourable to one who holds or has held an honourable office, though we do lower ourselves by giving it
to a fool or an idler merely because he is his father's son.
We do not lower ourselves by according an official cos-
tume and a proper address of respect to a judge. Let
Republicanism be simple; it must not carry its simplicity
to the extent of nakedness, if it means to keep its hold
on human sentiment. It must have, as the Common-

wealth under Cromwell had, a decent and symbolic state of its own.

Nor have we anything to say against family traditions. If a man has ancestors of whom he has reason to be proud, let him, by all means, cherish their memory, provided he does it without ostentation, and tries to live up to their example. It is good for the commonwealth that we should keep up every little prop of virtue which such associations afford. It is good that we should preserve bonds of sentiment which save us from being, as Burke said without such bonds we should be, flies of a summer. It is especially good in communities like ours, still unsettled and migratory, whose population shifts like sand. The passion of the Americans for tracing their English pedigrees has nothing in it irrational or at variance with republican principle, though it is to be feared that the demand too often produces the supply. It is a natural and healthy feeling, always supposing that it contents itself with what it can find in the genuine parish register and lets alone the Roll of Battle Abbey. The family Bible in which the little archives of the household used to be kept was a salutary as well as a pleasant institution. Of course pedigree-hunting has its weaknesses, among which is the fancy for tampering with names to give them an aristocratic sound. A Mr. Taylor who had grown rich and bought a country seat, changed his name to Tayleur. One day, being out with the hounds, he remarked to Lord Alvanley that a particular hound worked very well, and asked the hound's name. His name used, replied the wit, to be Jowler, but he has changed it to Jowleur.

It is scarcely needful to say that nothing is said against what is fancifully called the aristocracy of nature, that is, the aristocracy of mind. Leading intellects there are, and it is well for us that we should follow them, though not to the idolatrous excess of hero-worship taught by Carlyle. They may be allowed, as Schopenhauer says they ought, to wear the social insignia of their power, to stand in some measure apart from the rest of us, and commune more with their own thoughts than with other men. Only let them remember that above the aristocracy of intellect is still the aristocracy of worth, which is the same in a ploughman or mechanic as in Milton or Newton, and which retains its dignity undwarfed while the power of mind and all human power dwindles to nothing in face of the infinite universe. French Jacobins screamed against virtue itself as aristocratic, because it had pretensions to reverence, irrespective of the will of the divine people. This, like other bedlamite excesses of the Revolution, was a reaction from the reign of caste. While we renounce the worship of kings and nobles, let us not fall into the worship of the people, that is, of our aggregate selves.

There are false applications of the word aristocracy, and false claims about the existence of the thing in

these democratic communities. A trained and permanent civil service is sometimes denounced as an aristocracy, though it has nothing in it hereditary or
aristocratic in any way. This prejudice, again, is the
shadow of caste lingering on the public mind. We are
still, even on this continent, in the penumbra of feudal
institutions. Bureaucratic a permanent civil service
may become, though hardly without an autocratic government behind it. There is more reason in the dread
of a standing army as aristocratic. Military men are
apt to form a caste. Let our military men bear this in
mind, and take care not to make our people think that
they will be fostering Toryism and Jingoism, or anything that will dragoon the community, if they are
liberal to our volunteers.

Etymologically, aristocracy means the government of
the best. It was the aim of political philosophy among
the Greeks to form at the head of the State a body of
citizens trained to perfection in body and mind, and
dedicated wholly to the practice of virtue, so as to real-
ize the statuesque and somewhat haughty ideal of excellence set before us in Aristotle's "Ethics." To this object
were to be sacrificed not only the slaves who did the
coarse work of every ancient State, but the bulk of
the citizens, for the aristocrat was not to touch trade,
handicrafts, or anything meaner than war. This was a
Greek philosopher's dream, such as cannot even be

dreamed in a modern commonwealth. But what we call an aristocracy—that is, an order of privilege without personal merit—a Greek would have called, not an aristocracy, but an oligarchy. He would have looked with disdain on the French *noblesse* or the English peerage as having nothing to do with intrinsic excellence, dedication to a high calling, or the pursuit of a noble ideal.

Of historical aristocracies there have been more than one kind. The primitive aristocracies of the Greek and Italian Republics were privileged bodies of old settlers, with a clannish organization, keeping the new settlers out of the pale of the commonwealth. The old settlers at Rome were the patricians; the new settlers were the plebeians ; and the constitutional history of early Rome is the long struggle of the plebeians to break down the pale of privilege and make themselves full members of the State. The later Roman aristocracy, that which by its resolute and unswerving counsels gave such steadiness to the policy of the conquering Republic, was a mixed aristocracy of wealth, family, and official rank, the official rank being obtained legally at least by popular election. It was the images of ancestors who had held high office, not merely " tenth transmitters of a foolish face," that the Roman grandee kept in his hall, and that were borne in his funeral procession. Again, there was the Venetian aristocracy. This was a close order of privileged families whose names were inscribed in the Golden Book. But the young nobles in the palmy days of Venice at least, besides serving the State in war, were, unlike the members of the House of Lords, laboriously trained in administrative duty. This aristocracy gave Venice internal peace and security for six centuries, while all was faction and revolution around her. But its government was dark, and often cruel, and the well-being which it secured was commercial and material. Ruskin's religious and virtuous Venice is not the Venice of history, not even of that period of history in which "the Stones of Venice" were laid.

The aristocracy with which we have to do, and which faintly and fitfully tries to propagate itself here, is an offspring of the feudal aristocracy of the Middle Ages. But it is a bastard offspring. The feudal aristocracy was an organizing force in its day. The lord, though half-barbarian and often bad, was no idler or sybarite; he was the active head of the rural community, its magistrate in peace, its captain in war. In the absence of any central administration, there was no way of holding society together, or bringing the national force into the field, but such delegation of power to local authorities. The fiefs were not mere estates, but offices, and offices so hard that, as Stubbs tells us, the lives of the holders were shortened by toil and care, as well as by war. The forms of public duty attached to fiefs were not swept away till the reign of Charles II., when the landowners

purchased their abolition of the Crown, making the
nation pay the price by an excise duty. Not a few of
the barons in the Middle Ages left castle, wife, the joys
of the chase, and the song of the troubadour in the fes-
tive hall, to march to Syria in defence of Christian civilization against the inrolling tide of Mahometan conquest,
and noble names are in the roll of Crecy, Poictiers, and
Agincourt. The nobles seem to have pretty freely ad-
mitted merit of the military kind at least into their
circle, and a humble squire like Nesle Loring, winning
his nobility on the battle-field, could wear the Garter
which is now the perquisite of grandees, and which one
of them said he prized as the only thing nowadays not
given by merit. In the House of Lords the barons
mingled with bishops and abbots raised often from the
lowest rank, who usually formed more than half the
House. The pride of mere birth, apart from power or distinction, seems rather to belong to a decadence, in which
nothing but pedigrees remain. Of the comrades of William of Normandy, in fact, many could not have prided
themselves on their birth, though they might on their
strong arms. The sentiment does not meet you much, as
far as I know, in writers of the feudal period, at least
in the writers of its earlier and healthier portion. Fiefs
were not, at first, hereditary, but naturally became so ;
indeed, if the sovereign had kept the power of appoint-
ing anew on each vacancy his power would have been
overwhelming. It was by the security of their tenure

that the barons were enabled to act, in a rude and rather blind fashion, as the prospective trustees of liberty, and to rough-hew the British Constitution. Nominees of the Crown would never have extorted the Great Charter or founded the House of Commons. Evolution has taught us to do justice to every institution and organization in its own time and place. But feudal aristocracy carried in itself the seeds of anarchy and suicide. The anarchy was always breaking out, and the suicide came in the Wars of the Roses. By that time the day of modern society had dawned.

Out of the wreck of the feudal baronage rose the new aristocracy of the Tudors. This is the real date of the modern English nobility ; no higher source can it claim, in spite of the Norman pedigrees which used to figure in the peerage, till they were taken in hand by Professor Freeman. Some of the old feudal houses survived, though with a character changed by the new conditions, and the heir of one of them, a genuine Norman by lineage, was some time ago detected in cheating at cards. The Tudor aristocracy was an aristocracy of court minions, partakers in Henry's plunder of the Church, and accomplices in his judicial murders. Its ownership of Church lands is largely the account of its attachment to Protestantism and of such Liberalism as it ever displayed. This influence lasted even down to the days of the Stuart pretenders. About the first act of the new aristocracy was the judicial murder of the Protector Somerset, who, though not the best of men, had shown a disposition to take the part of the people against upstart oppression. About its next act was the betrayal, under Mary, of the national religion, which it sold to the Pope for a quiet title to the Church lands, while peasants and mechanics went to the stake for their faith.

The new aristocracy in England did not become an aristocracy of courtiers, like the French *noblesse* under Louis XIV. It became an aristocracy of great landowners with rural palaces, and thus retained its influence. Good landowners, happily, no doubt some of them have always been. But the order ceased to be an order of duty. Its political organ, the House of Lords, became an organ of privilege and reaction. Instead of extorting any more Great Charters, it blocked the Habeas Corpus Act. It never stood between the people and Tudor tyranny. It absolutely grovelled at the feet of the monster Henry VIII. When resistance to arbitrary government came it was from Puritanism in the House of Commons. In the time of Charles I. a few peers showed by their conduct that ascendancy of conviction over interest which exceptionally distinguished the time; but most of them, after opposing Strafford, whom they regarded with jealousy as an upstart encroaching on their power and Laud, whose Romanizing tendencies threatened their Church lands, as soon as they saw that reform was becoming dangerous to privilege, showed the natural bias of their order, and went over to the Crown. The Lords did not protest against the tyranny of Charles II. in his later days; nor did they protest against the murderous cruelties of James II., or even against his political usurpations, till their own interests were manifestly threatened. Not a voice was raised in the House of Lords, as far as we know, against the Bloody Assize or the murder of Alice Lisle. There was antagonism between aristocracy and Stuart absolutism, as well as between lay privilege and priestly ambition, besides the fear, still present, of an attempt on the part of the ecclesiastics to disturb the great Houses in the possession of the Church lands.

After the final overthrow of the Stuarts, the German dynasty being weak and the system of rotten boroughs, which gave the Lords the nomination of a great part of the House of Commons, having been left untouched at the Revolution, the aristocracy was in power. What followed? A reign of corruption more profound and shameless than there ever was seen in the United States. It is not suspected, I believe, that any treaty has been carried through the American Senate like the Treaty of Paris by bribery. English politics were a mere struggle between different aristocratic cliques for a vast mass of public pelf. Chatham rose above all this, but Chatham was the man of the people. The head of the aristocracy was Newcastle, of all jobbers and wirepullers the most contemptible. Aristocratic morals were on a par with aristocratic politics, and the contagion of both spread among the people.

That the House of Lords has acted as the sober second-thought of the nation, correcting the rashness of the popular House, is a mere fiction. Why, indeed, should a young Lord be less rash than an old Commoner ? The House of Lords has done nothing but block all change, as far as it dared, in the interest of privilege. It blocked not only Parliamentary reform, but religious justice, the freedom of the press, personal liberty, and even measures of mere humanity, such as the reform of the criminal law and the abolition of the slave trade. It blocked Parliamentary reform till the nation was brought to the verge of revolution, when it succumbed to fear. Had it possessed wisdom and courage it might have usefully modified the change. The House of Lords has never initiated a reform or improvement of firstrate importance. Its legislative barrenness is almost as notable as that of our Senate. True, the great Whig Houses took the lead in the struggle for Parliamentary reform. They had been out of power for half-a-century, and had contracted a strong spirit of opposition, which indeed they carried to an unpatriotic excess in their anti-national sympathy with Napoleon. But it was not in the cause of Parliamentary reform that they had forfeited place; it was

through the coalition of the Crown and the people, provoked by the unprincipled coalition of Fox and North ;
nor had they when in power shown any disposition to re-
resign their rotten boroughs, or in any way to purify the
representation. They had their tradition of 1688, but
it had not been found worth much when they were in
power under George II.

Hereditary estates being the indispensable basis of
hereditary power, the entrance to the House of Lords has
been ordinarily by the gate of wealth. Pitt said that any
man who had ten thousand a year had a right to be made
a peer if he pleased. All the Lord Chancellors have become peers as a matter of course ; but then a Lord Chan-
cellor is sure to have made a fortune at the bar. The
House can hardly be said to have been the national tem-
ple of honour. Leicester, Elizabeth's scoundrel lover,
was a peer ; Walsingham, Drake, and Raleigh, who saved
the country, were not. Under the Stuarts peerages
were put up for sale, and the payments were entered in
the books of the Exchequer. Even purchase was a better title than that of the minions of James I. A notable
addition was made to the peerage by the harem of Charles
II. Twelve peers were created at once by Bolingbroke
to carry the treaty of Utrecht, which, besides betraying
the fruits of national victory in a long war, involved infamous treachery to an ally. Pitt immensely increased
the peerage by creations bestowed almost always for mere

party services. Nelson, it is true, going into action, cried, "A peerage or Westminster Abbey!" But then he thought of the coronet on his own brow, not on that of the tenth transmitter. After the battle of the Nile, Pitt, who could lavish the highest grades of the peerage on nonentities, threw the lowest to Nelson. He said that nobody would ask whether Nelson was a viscount or a baron. In other words, the title bore no relation to the service or the glory.

The war against revolutionary France was commenced in the interest of privilege. In the war the peers showed the tenacity for which aristocracies are famous. But they threw the burden on the people. They made no patriotic sacrifice themselves, gave up not a single sinecure, cut down not one plethoric salary. The people were pressed into the navy, decoyed into the army, shed their blood under such commanders as the Duke of York, were starved by war prices of food. The peers sat at home revelling in the high rents which war prices produced, and lauding themselves for their firmness of purpose. The seamen, on whom the salvation of the country depended, were defrauded of their pay and rations till they were driven to a mutiny which brought the · nation to the verge of destruction. Napier said that the British army fought under the cold shade of an aristocracy, and he might have extended his remark with emphasis to the British navy. In the glories of either arm, the aristocratic Government had little part.

Nothing is more sad or more significant than the state
of the criminal law when the aristocracy was at the
height of its power. ·It showed a hideous lavishness of
plebeian blood. The number of capital offences amounted
at last to one hundred and sixty, the offences being almost all those of the poor, while the rich indulged in
duelling and any other vice to which they had a mind.
For a soldier or sailor to beg without a license was death,
though it was lawful for people of quality to plunder
the public.   Shoplifting was death.   A child not ten
years old was once under sentence for it. A poor woman,
whose husband had been pressed as a sailor, took something from a shop to prevent her from starving. She
was condemned to be hanged, and was carried to Tyburn
with a child at her breast.   Stealing from the person
was death.   An acquaintance of my own told me that
through his access to the Home Secretary he had been
the means of saving from the gallows a man who had
taken something from the person of another in a tipsy
brawl.   Romilly's efforts in the cause of mercy were
again and again defeated in the Lords, and in the
majority against abolishing the punishment of death for
a petty theft, there voted seven bishops.   So infectious
was the air of that hall. Democracy has had fits of
sanguinary madness, such as the French Reign of Terror,
but when it is itself it is humane. Not that the noble-
men and ladies either of France or England were cruel.
There was nothing cruel in Madame de Sévigné, though

she speaks in one of her letters with graceful levity of peasants being hanged by the score or broken on the wheel. It was simply that she and her caste at heart hardly recognized the link of a common humanity between them and the peasant or anyone who was not noble. Known to all is Carlyle's French Duchess, who said that God would think twice before He damned a man of quality. The Duchess of Buckingham, in answer to an invitation from the Methodist Lady Huntingdon to attend her chapel, wrote, "The doctrines of the Methodist preachers are most repulsive and strongly tinctured with impertinence towards their superiors in perpetually endeavouring to level the ranks and do away with all distinctions. It is monstrous to be told you have a heart as sinful as the common wretches that crawl on the earth."

The slackness of the attendance in the House of Lords while London is full of peers amusing themselves has been a constant scandal. Great questions are debated and settled in a discreditably thin House. In vain the better members of the order have preached duty. There are bright exceptions, men whom nature has made of her finest clay ; but as a rule duty has not its seat in the bosoms of those who are brought up to wealth which they have not earned, and to rank which they have not won. Heredity, considering that it is a real force in the animal kingdom, seems to prevail wonderfully little in the mental succession of men. "All great men have

fools for their sons ; you see what a fool that son of mine
is," was reported to have been the naïve exclamation of
a distinguished personage in England.   But the horse or
the dog of generous breed is not spoiled by aristocratic
training.   Horace sings that the valiant are the sons of
valiant sires, and that the eagle never begets the dove.
The eaglet will not be worthy of his sire if you bring
him up like a Strasburg goose.   The highest meed of
admiration is due to the man who has been able to resist
the influences which surround the coroneted cradle of a
peer.   The wonder is not that so many of the British
aristocracy have been and are content to be mere men
of pleasure, but that so many have tried and are trying
to be something more.

The French aristocracy, after its reign of insolence and
vice, when the day of trial came, ran away and left its
king to the guillotine.   The British aristocracy, happily,
is not likely to be tried in so tragic a way, and if it were,
would show a better front.   But its situation is at this
moment critical, and it does not seem to rise to the emer-
gency.   We hear of efforts to make up for the fall of
rents by speculations in land, and sometimes in American
heiresses, but not of increased effort in the performance
of either social or parliamentary duty.   Nor, unhappily,
does the number of social scandals decrease.

I fail to see what good British aristocracy has done the
community since it ceased to be an order of feudal duty

and became an order of mere rank and privilege. The most glorious hour in the national annals since the Middle Ages seems to me to be that of the Commonwealth, when aristocracy was out of the way. History, as I read it, offers no assurance that national character can draw any genuine nobility, or national councils any true wisdom, from that spring. But let England look to this. We do not presume to interfere with her political development. If she thinks that the retention of aristocracy for a while can save her from plunging into a democracy of passion, demagogism, and faction, practical wisdom will council her to retain it without a regard for democratic theory. But here hereditary rank has never had a home, and never can have one. It can only misdirect aspiration and pervert development. To inoculate our body politic with it is to inoculate the living from a corpse. Even in Europe the hereditary principle is dead at the root. Hereditary monarchy lingers in life because it has been divested of all power. But the House of Lords, I believe, is now the only hereditary assembly left, though in some other assemblies there is an hereditary element. The Australian Confederation calls itself a commonwealth, and a commonwealth, according to the dictionaries and vocabularies, is something different from a kingdom. The grand type of hereditary royalty, the monarchy of the Bourbons in France, has been replaced by a republic. To fancy that the intrusion of the hereditary principle can give stability to our institutions is absurd.

Stability we want indeed, but we must look for it elsewhere.

Grades of social condition, differences between rich and
poor, employer and employed, learned and unlearned,
skilled and unskilled, there are, and unfortunately will be
till society undergoes a transmutation which is not likely
to come in our time, whatever social possibilities there
may be in the womb of the future. The social organism,
like everything else in the universe, so far as we can see,
is full of imperfections. But we need not make matters
worse by drawing artificial lines. Hereditary rank does
draw such lines. It has exercised a bad influence in this
way on the whole frame of society in aristocratic countries. Exclusiveness runs all down the social grade,
and the farmer's wife is "my lady" to the wife of the
hired man.

Respect for rank, we are always told, is inherent in man.
Surely not respect for rank wholly unconnected with
merit or service. Surely not respect for the rank of a
fool or a profligate. This has been engrafted on human
nature by the aristocratic system and has now struck
pretty deep roots, but it is no more a part of human
nature than any other folly or baseness. There is a well-
known story of a man who bet that he would slap a perfect stranger on the back in Pall Mall without offending
him, and won his bet by telling the stranger, when he
turned upon him in a fury, that he had taken him for a

nobleman of his acquaintance whom he wonderfully re-
sembled. The sentiment typified by this story, though
common, we may hope is not ineradicable. It is true
that American Republicans often show it in an extreme
form; but are they not always ashamed of it ? The love
of titles is natural enough ? But once more, against titles
there is nothing to be said, so long as they denote genuine
service of any kind to the community. It is not likely
that those who care most for them, or for any external
distinction, will be the most high-minded and truly noble
of mankind. The authority by which they are awarded
never can be like that of which the voice is heard in a
man's own breast. Still the love of them is natural and
they have their use. We have only to take care that
they are not multiplied to an absurd extent, that we have
not more honourables than men without that handle to
their names, more colonels than civilians, more Grand
Arches than simple mortals, more bashaws with three
tails than people without any tails at all.

Feudal titles are one of the social influences which
combine to give a false direction to what, if the phrase is
not pedantic, may be called our political æsthetics. So
long as we have bodily senses and our minds are im-
pressed through them, it will really be of consequence
that the outward form and vesture of government should
be truly symbolic of its character ; that it should have a
majesty, however democratic and simple, of its own. We

miss that mark when we try to reproduce the antique
pomp of an old feudal monarchy without its genuine
magnificence, and without the historical associations by
which its obsoleteness is redeemed. You will know what
I mean if you will recall to mind the account which was
given us of the opening of Parliament the other day.
Plainly, the ceremony was a travesty of the opening of
Parliament at Westminster, with its military parade, its
great officers of State glittering with decorations, and
its peeresses in full dress filling the gallery. The opening of the great council of the nation ought to be a
solemn act, but that is not the way to make it solemn.

Knighthood, as we began by saying, not being hereditary, is not properly aristocratic. King William IV. was
fond of making after-dinner speeches. On one occasion
he found himself seated between a Duke of Royal descent and a tradesman who had been knighted as Lord
Mayor. This gave him an opportunity of pointing out
that in England everything was open to merit. "On my
right," he said, "sits the Duke of Buckingham, with the
blood of the Plantagenets in his veins; on my left sits
Sir Somebody Something raised from the very dregs of
the people." But though not strictly aristocratic, knighthood is feudal, as the fees paid to the herald office testify
to the knight's cost. It carries with it aristocratic as well
as military associations. Surely a more appropriate decoration might be conferred on a portly financier, a veteran

politician, or a venerable man of science, than that which
was borne by Sir Galahad and the Knights of the Round
Table. Some of the leading men of letters and science
in England are understood to have declined the honour.
Perhaps the effort of self-denial was not great, since their
beneficent eminence would have shared the distinction
with almost domestic services performed to the court.
But a feeling of the inappropriateness of the title probably mingled with the well-founded conviction that their
merit stood in need of no title at all. Among ourselves
men worthy of all distinction in different lines, men
whom this community would itself have delighted to
honour, have accepted knighthoods. Others not less
worthy have refused them, and for the sacrifice involved
in the refusal our gratitude is due.

There is an objection to honours not conferred by the
community in which the man lives and acts. They
divide his allegiance. If he is a politician he steers the
ship of State with an eye always turned to the country
from which his honour comes, like those ecclesiastical
statesmen of the Middle Ages, who steered the national
barque with an eye always turned to Rome. If his aspirations are social they are diverted from Canada to
Mayfair. This is no slight evil. The tendency of those
who have earned wealth on this side of the Atlantic to
spend it on the other side is great enough, without the
additional stimulus of a special affiliation to British

society. The inducements are obvious enough and the
tendency is most excusable. Society in the Old Country
is more brilliant, services are better, the means of enjoying wealth in every way are greater. But here is the
post of social duty, and, as pleasure without duty palls,
of genuine happiness. These are not times in which
those who ought to be active leaders of society can afford
to be absentees. If our municipal affairs, among other
things, do not go right, the reason is, in part, that the
right men do not take hold of them ; and the reason of
that again, in part, is, that our social chiefs are apt to be
almost as much citizens of London as of Toronto.

Honours awarded by a distant authority will sometimes be awarded in ignorance. I have heard a Colonial
Secretary admit that his office in one instance had made
a serious mistake. It may be said with some force, on
the other hand, that titles not in the gift of the party
leader cannot, like Senatorships, be swept into the party
fund. On this point we should feel more assured if we
knew more about the process of recommendation, which
at present is behind the veil. We unfortunately know
it to be possible that, where the community has pronounced deserved censure, a title of honour may be conferred, as if for the express purpose of nullifying the
public verdict and trampling on the justice of the nation.

Can it be said that as a matter of fact titles of chivalry
have brought a chivalrous sense of honour to the breasts

of their possessors, thence to radiate over the community
at large ? To that question the history of the Pacific
Railway Scandal is the answer. Who have done more to
corrupt public morality, to lower the tone of public life,
to saturate the country with corruption, to degrade the
public press into an organ of ignoble passion and a dag-
ger for the assassination of character, than men who are
described as appearing at the meeting of Parliament
glittering with golden embroidery and with the Grand
Cross of an order of chivalry on their breasts ? Who
make war on their political opponents by slanderous
charges of conspiracy and treason? Who accept the
services of spies and use letters obtained by dishonour-
able means ? If we were asked to say whose name,
among all our politicians, has been most associated with
the practice of corruption, are we sure that the bearer
of an hereditary title would not be the man ? If an
equivocal trade was denounced in Parliament, would you
be surprised beyond measure to hear that it was by the
heir to a title that the trade was being plied ?

To us the models of aristocratic character are our
Governors-General. High specimens of all that is best
in their order on the whole they have been. Being con-
stitutionally deprived of all real power, they have seldom
had even a chance of showing of what metal they were
made. But when they have had a chance, has heroic
self-sacrifice been displayed ? Have we even looked for
anything of the kind ? When a Governor-General has

been called upon to shield accused Ministers by taking an inquiry out of the hands of the Grand Inquest of the nation and transferring it to a Commission appointed by the accused, to consent to the lawless dismissal of his own representative for the gratification of party vengeance, to make an appointment to the judiciary at which the whole legal profession cried shame, to allow a tricky and perfidious use to be made of the prerogative of dissolution, has it been thought possible that he should say, I know my constitutional position, and on all questions of policy I will follow the advice of my Ministers, but I will not lend my name to dishonour, and if you force me, I will go home. *Noblesse oblige* is not true. *Noblesse absout* would be nearer the truth. A man of rank is apt to feel, and with reason, that though he may not do what would be expected of untitled men, his rank and position are secure. The recent dissolution of Parliament for a party purpose has shown us too plainly that the presence of a man of rank as the head of our polity is no security for the maintenance of public right or for the integrity of our institutions.

These Imperial decorations are naturally dear to Imperialists, who see in them a remaining link of the political connection. This reason, of course, will not weigh, or rather it will weigh in the opposite scale, with those who see in political connection only a survival of the obsolete belief that colonists remain personal liegemen of the monarch of the mother country, and are

convinced that the whole course of things has been
tending, and will continue to tend, towards Independence. My respected friend, Principal Grant, in a
review which he has done me the honour to write of a
little work of mine, says that it is impossible that an
Englishman, especially one brought up in so narrow a
place as the University of Oxford, and I suppose he
would add, on a study so contracting to the mind as
History, after being in Canada only twenty years, can
understand Canadian sentiment. British-Canadian sentiment I presume he means, for he can hardly think that
the sentiments of British and French-Canadians are
alike occult and at the same time perfectly identical.
How comes it, then, I would ask, that the words of a
Governor-General are oracles, even though he may be an
Oxford man and have not been in Canada twenty days?
Is this again a case of that respect for rank inherent in
human nature, and which made the man in our story
feel so charmed on being told that he had been mistaken
for a duke? A more important question is, if there is
such a gulf between the sentiment of the Englishman
and that of the Canadian, what use there can be in
struggling against geography to keep England and
Canada in political connection with each other? Sentiment means character, tendencies, aspirations. If in
these the communities are two, what political machinery
or gimcrackery will ever make them one? Nativism
and Imperialism do not hang well together. If I were

not disqualified for judging, on the grounds assigned by
my friend, I should say that I do see a difference
between the political character of the Englishman and
that of the Canadian, and that while it is partly the difference between the citizen of a nation and the citizen of
a dependency, it is partly also the difference between a
citizen of the Old and a citizen of the New World. The
stronger an affection is the less one feels inclined to
parade it, and I do not want to be always shouting on
the house-top that I love Old England. I leave that to
loyalists on their road to Ottawa to demand an increase
of the duties on British goods. But that I do love Old
England, no one in England, I believe, of my acquaintance doubts. I must confess, however, that I do not
value baronetcies and knighthoods any the more on
account of their tendency to perpetuate a bond, the dis-
advantages and dangers of which are every day becoming more apparent, while its dissolution, if brought about
in kindness, would only strengthen the bond of the
heart. I am one of those who go, in a certain sense,
beyond Imperial Federation, inasmuch as I desire a
moral federation not only of the forty millions but of
the hundred millions of the English-speaking race, leaving each section of the race to regulate its political institutions and its commercial affairs in accordance with its
own interests and the circumstances of its own case. If
this is treason, it is treason from which some Englishmen who were supposed to be good patriots and good
servants of the Crown have not been free.

JINGOISM.[*]

INGOISM, I suppose, is a word now natural-
ized in our language. It is the only word
we have corresponding to the French "Chauvinism." It seems that Chauvinism is derived from the name of Colonel Chauvin, a fire-
eating patriot in a French comedy. Jingoism is
derived, as you know, from the words of the stave sung
in the London music halls when Great Britain was quar-
relling with Russia:

" We don't want to fight, but by Jingo if we do,
   We've got the men, we've got the ships, we've got the money too,"

which, when Lord Beaconsfield brought the Sepoys to
Malta, was parodied thus:

" We don't want to fight, but by Jingo if we do,
   We'll stay at home at ease ourselves and send the mild Hindoo."

That is just what the warriors of the music hall do.
Glorious with the excitement of the beer and the fid-
dling, they send other men by their votes to the field of
slaughter and again swell with pride as they read the
tale of carnage in the newspaper. Yet if they could once

* Delivered before the Young Men's Liberal Club, Toronto, Nov, 9th, 1891,

see the wreck of a battlefield or the contents of a field-hospital, the spectacle might counteract the effects of the beer and fiddles.

All honour to the character of the true soldier. Nobody, I suppose, who professes Christianity would say that he wants more wars than can be helped. There are some even fastidious enough to think that blessings of colours by the clergy, and trophies hung up in churches are rather difficult to reconcile with the Sermon on the Mount. But we cannot help seeing that the time is yet far distant when, according to the Prophet, the lion will eat straw like the ox. Some of the old causes of war are nearly, if not wholly, extinct. We are not likely to have more wars for religion or for dynastic right. Bare-faced wars of conquest will hardly be waged again by civilized governments: the last were waged not by a civilized government, but by a Corsican* and his heir. On the other hand, Protectionism, coming back to us from the tomb of medieval ignorance, may revive international hatred and set us again fighting to destroy our neighbour's harvest lest it should add to the plenty of our own. Then there are wars of race and revived nationality, such as the Pan-Slavonic crusades of Russia and the War of Hungarian independence. There are rights still to be defended, powers of violence and wrong

---

* The late Lord Russell used to say that when he had an interview with Napoleon at Elba upon his mentioning war the dominant passion gleamed in Napoleon's eye

still to be restrained. To disarm all civilized nations
would be to put the world at the mercy of the bar-
barians. Besides, order may sometimes require to be
upheld against anarchy, and no one upholds it so well as
the regular soldier who does not share the political
passions, and fires only at the word of command. Arbi-
tration has done much to supersede war, and it may do
more, but it cannot do all. Pride or cupidity will sometimes admit no arbitrator but the sword. All Europe is
in arms, rumours of impending hostilities come to us by
every other mail, and though the dread of a conflict so
terrible as this would be has hitherto been great enough
to prolong a precarious and uneasy peace, it seems as if
from mere tension and the intolerable pressure of the
expense, one of the powers must some day break. Meantime who does not pay homage to the military virtues,
to the soldier's contempt of pain and death, his endur-
ance of fatigue and hardship, his loyalty to duty, his self-
devotion, his noble submission to discipline, and the
chivalrous forbearance towards conquered foes, by which
he has made modern war a great school of humanity? In
an age in which respect for authority is weak, and what
is called self-government is being carried to the verge of
anarchy, military discipline is an element which civilization itself could ill afford to lose. Nor can commercial
communities, with their stock exchanges and their gold
rooms, afford to part with the army as a school of
honour. Amidst all the suspicions of corruption which

were abroad in the United States at the time of the Civil War, no shadow, as far as I remember, fell on the characters of the West Point men. We have learned to talk with horror of a government of musketeers and pikemen. Is it certain that the Commonwealth would be worse off in the hands of musketeers and pikemen, like those of Cromwell, the flower of the citizens in arms for a great cause, than it is in the hands of the political bosses and wirepullers who rule it now?

Englishmen of my age have heard not only the stories of Inkerman and Sobraon but those of the Peninsula and Waterloo from the lips of men who fought there. There was no swagger or fanfaronade about those men. They did not even betray a love of war. Lord Hardinge used always to speak of war with horror, like Marlborough, who after Malplaquet, prayed that he might never be in another battle. Yet Lord Hardinge was the Governor-General of India who doffed his viceroyalty to serve against the Sikhs at Sobraon. Returning from famous fields, the British soldier marches to his barracks with the simplicity of veterans amidst public emotion rather deep than loud. Simplicity is the garb of genuineness. Strange to say, it is not in the old military countries but in these industrial and intellectual communities of ours that the passion for martial show most prevails. Is it that we want to avoid being set down as shopkeepers, or that there is something feminine in industrial character which

disposes it to "flirt with scarlet and coquet with
steel ?" The Volunteer movement in England was no
mere pastime. It was a serious effort called forth by
a danger which lowered from the dark councils of the
French Emperor, and of the reality of which there has
since been conclusive proof. The cause of our delight
in the pageantry, perhaps, is simply our ignorance of the
grim realities of war.

All honour once more to the character of the true soldier, and above all when he is fighting in defence of his
country. Country is a circle of affection intermediate
between the family and mankind, with which few are
yet cosmopolitan enough to suppose that we can dispense.
But we should all say, I suppose, that the love of country
must be kept within the limits of morality. American
Jingoes, at the time of the aggression on Mexico, said that
'they were for the country right or wrong.' That was a
doctrine of devils. It was also a doctrine of fools; for
the nation which acted on it would soon have the world
for its enemy, and would find that, though morality is
not so strong as we could wish, it is stronger than any
robber-horde. Somebody argued the other day that a
nation which hurt other nations in promoting its own interests was no more to be blamed than the hunter who
killed game for his dinner. But we are becoming awake
to the fact that a nation cannot hurt other nations without hurting itself, the nations being, like men, a com-

munity and members one of another. Among the plea-
santest memories of my life I reckon my intercourse with
Joseph Mazzini. Mazzini passionately loved his country, if ever man did, and he kindled in the breasts of Italian youth the fire of patriotism which set his Italy free.
But he was not a Jingo any more than he was a Jacobin.
He was a man of deeply religious nature, and his aspirations were thoroughly moral. With lifelong devotion he
served the nation, but he regarded the nation itself as
the servant and organ of humanity. I have always looked upon the spirit which he infused as the main cause of
the comparatively calm and moderate character of Italian
revolution. Such a patriotism will display itself in noble
ways. It will be seen in working, not in blustering, for
the country, in honestly telling her the truth at whatever cost, not in offering to her the poisonous sacrifice of
lies. You brag and gasconade, and you traduce your
fellow-citizens for not bragging and gasconading like you.
Then comes the Census, and brag and gasconade are in
the dust.

Put up monuments to the heroes of Queenston
Heights and Lundy's Lane—again we say we gladly
will. The heroes of Queenston indeed have already a
monument not less creditable to Canadian taste than
were their deeds to Canadian valour. But we will
gladly set up a monument to the heroes of Lundy's
Lane. Only let it be like that monument at Quebec,

a sign at once of gratitude and of reconciliation, not of
the meanness of unslaked hatred. We cannot by any
demonstrations appropriate to ourselves the glory of
those who fought at Queenston Heights or Lundy's Lane,
and why should we forever hug the quarrel which by
those who did fight, if they were generous as well as
brave, would probably have been long since laid aside.
The soldiers of the North and South fought at Gettys-
burg not less desperately than the English on the north
and those on the south of the Line fought at Lundy's
Lane, yet they could meet again the other day as breth-
ren on the field of the battle. Let us erect a monument
to all the brave who fell at Lundy's Lane, and invite the
Americans to the unveiling. The heir of many a Canadian who fought on that field is now on the American
side of the Line.

It is well, moreover, that we, an industrial and we
hope moral and enlightened community, should remember that death on the field of battle is not the only
honourable death, and that many a life besides that of
the soldier is sacrificed, though without blare of trumpet
or pomp of war, at the call of public duty. Why not
put up monuments to the physician or the hospital
nurse who dies in braving contagion, to the fireman who
perishes in rescuing people from a fire, to the captain
of a vessel or the driver of an engine who loses his own
life in saving those of the passengers in his ship or

train ? Perhaps lives are sometimes offered up to the
common weal less visibly yet not less really than even
these.

Put up monuments by all means at Queenston Heights
and Lundy's Lane, but do not bid us celebrate Ridgeway. Queenston Heights and Lundy's Lane were
battles and victories, though our victory at Lundy's
Lane was hardly won. Ridgeway was neither a battle
nor a victory. It was a miserable affair all round. Nor
was it an American attack on Canada : it was an attack
of Irish Fenians on a dependency of Great Britain. The
American Government might have stopped it more
promptly, considering that through the whole of the
Civil War Canada had scrupulously done her international duty ; but some allowance must be made for the
irritation caused among people struggling for national
existence by the hostile bearing of a powerful party in
England and by the taunts of the British press. It was
right that those who had fallen in the service of the
country should receive honourable burial. But surely
over those graves the grass might be allowed to grow.
When after the lapse of a quarter of a century such a
memory is laboriously revived, who can doubt the
motive and who can respect it ?

Once more we must earnestly protest against the attempt to use the public schools as nurseries of party
passion, which has been repeated since my first lecture.

Such a course is not only uncivic, it is unpatriotic, for
patriotism can never run counter to public right. It is
even unmanly : the mind of a child is defenceless : if we
want to propagate our opinions or sentiments let us seek
entrance for them into the minds of men. The object
cannot be doubtful. For why should the anniversaries
of victories gained in war with the Americans be picked
out as the occasion for stirring up the patriotism of our
children ? Are there no other victories in British history ? Why should the list be confined to the victories
of war at all ? For an industrial nation, has not peace
her victories as well as war ? If a party use is to be
made of the public schools, ratepayers will be looking not
only to the elections of Mayor and Aldermen, but to
those of school trustees, which at present most of them
allow to go by default. Hoisting of flags, chanting of
martial songs, celebration of battle anniversaries, erec-
tion of military monuments, decoration of patriotic
graves, arming and reviewing of the very children in our
public schools—if Jingoism finds itself in need of all
these stimulants, we shall begin to think that it must be
sick.

What do our Jingoes want ? Do they really wish to
provoke a war with the United States ? From their language and that of the leaders of their party at elections,
we might think they did. Have they measured the
chances of such a war, even supposing each of them to

be a Paladin? Have they counted its cost? Their
thoughts are full of the glories of 1812. Have they considered how much the invader's resources and his power
of bringing them to bear have increased since that time?
Do they fancy that Canada is still a fortress of forests?
Have they provided for the defence of the great and un-
fortified cities which she had not in 1812, but now has
on her frontier open to the enemy's attack? They
reckon on the protection of the British army and fleet!
Does it not occur to them that the British army and fleet
may at the time have enough to do in protecting the
British shores? Suppose the British ironclads could
bombard American cities, do they think that the destruction of American cities would make up for the
wreck of Canadian industry and the desolation of Canadian homes? Have they even studied the history of the
War of 1812, marked how, as the struggle went on, the
Americans learned discipline, and noted how different
was their fighting at Lundy's Lane from what it had
been at Detroit or Chateauguay? Above all, let us ask
again, who are to be the enemy? Those million and
a half of Canadians and their children who are already
on the South of the Line and whose numbers are swelled
every year by the very flower of Canadian youth—are
they to be fired on by their own fathers and brothers?
French Canada, through the immense migration into
the adjoining States, is now actually astride the Line
—will the Northern half of it take arms against the

Southern half ? Will it do this if France is on the enemy's side ? We talk proudly of our flag, the symbol of
our nationality ; but the flag of Quebec is the tricolor.

In challenging the United States, our Jingoes always
assume that they have Great Britain behind them. But
they forget that in Great Britain there no longer reigns
an aristocracy able and willing to make war with the
blood and earnings of the people. The people have now
something to say to the question, and who that knows
anything of their present temper can imagine that they
would be ready, for any Canadian question, to go to war
with the United States ? Their feelings towards us are
as kindly as possible, but their interest in us is comparatively slight, especially since we have definitely re-·
nounced the commercial unity of the Empire, and laid
protective duties on British goods. There are two or
three English politicians who make Canada their speci-
alty, and are credited with understanding our affairs and
running us. But the British people, as a mass, hardly
ever turn their eyes this way.

It seems that nothing can conjure the spectre of
American aggression. We were once more told the other
day that we were lying under the colossal shadow of a
rapacious neighbour, whose greedy maw was gaping to
devour us. Colossal our neighbour and his shadow may
be, but where are the signs of his rapacity ? He has an
army of twenty-five thousand men, mainly employed in

fighting Indians. At the close of the Civil War the Americans had a vast and victorious army; they had also a great fleet; yet they showed no disposition to attack us. Let me say once more that I have been going among the Americans now for more than twenty years; I have held intercourse with people of all classes, parties, professions, characters and ages, including the youth of a University who are sure to speak as they feel. I never heard the slightest expression of a wish to aggress on Canada, or to force her into the Union. The motives for annexation which existed in the days of Slavery now exist no more. The fire-eating and aggressive spirit which Slavery bred, and which found utterance in the Ostend manifesto, departed with the institution which was its source. I do not doubt that by the Americans generally Canada would be welcomed if she came of her own accord. The union of this Continent is a natural aspiration, and surely one at least as rational, as moral and as beneficent, as those cravings of ambition which set the Powers of the Old World by the ears. But among the politicians there would be a strong minority against admission, because they are afraid that it would disturb their party combinations. I have heard some of them avow this in the plainest terms. Protectionism, moreover, is as narrow and selfish on that side as on ours, and would see the aspirations of this Continent or of mankind defeated rather than pull down a tariff wall. American councils are not dark, like those of a despot, that we

should be afraid of secret plots being hatched against us
at Washington. American councils are as open as our
own. If there were any design against us we should be
sure to be apprised of it at the next political picnic.

The McKinley Act, we are persistently told, is directed against us, and intended to coerce us into the
resignation of our independence. My friend, Sir George
Baden-Powell, repeats that cry. Is the Act directed
against us more than against England, France, Germany,
or any of the other nations which suffer by it and are
protesting against it? If it was a stroke of policy for
the fulfilment of a national ambition, why did the nation
condemn it by an overwhelming vote at the polls? Why
in that campaign did we never hear the Act defended
as a well-concerted measure of aggrandizement? Cannot our Jingoes, who are mostly Protectionists, believe
in the existence among our neighbours also of a Protectionism inspired by no loftier or subtler motive than
commercial greed? Why do they abuse the McKinley
Act at all? It is a splendid illustration of their own
principles. They ought to hail it as a fresh and glorious
proof that the blessed light of Monopoly is spreading
over the world and chasing away the dark shadows of
commercial and industrial freedom.

If our Jingoes do not mean war, what is the use of
stirring up hatred? Whatever our political relations,
either to the United States or to Great Britain, may be

destined to be, it is certain that we must share this continent with the Americans, that our interests must be
bound up in a hundred ways with those of our powerful
neighbours, and that on our being on good terms with
them our security and prosperity must largely depend.
Say as positively as you please that you are opposed to
political union, the Americans will not resent your desire
to remain independent. The love of independence in itself commands their respect. But why persist in saying
things which they may resent, and which may lead to a
fatal quarrel? England, amidst all her perils and em-
barrassments in Europe and Asia, is trying to settle for
us the Fisheries and the Behring Sea questions at Washington. This is the time which a Canadian Government
and its party choose to make our platforms ring, and to
cover our walls at election time, with groundless denunciations of American ambition and gross insults to the
American name and flag. England herself meantime is
courting American friendship, doing her best to efface the
memories of the *Alabama*, and all that was untoward at
that time, putting up the bust of Longfellow in Westminster Abbey, celebrating memorial services for Grant and
Garfield, and strewing flowers on Lowell's grave. My
friend, Mr. O. A. Howland, has shown in a very interesting
way how Shelburne, the most enlightened statesman of
his day, tried, after the severance of the American Colonies from the mother country, to bury the quarrel, and
to get back to something like the family footing; and

Shelburne had for his colleague Pitt, whom nobody will
accuse of lack of patriotism or of national pride. We are
too British for the British themselves.

If Americanophobia were not too long a word, if it
were as easily pronounced as hydrophobia, perhaps it
might have been the title of this Address. For Americanophobia is practically the shape which all our Jingoism takes. No Englishman—and he who addresses you
is an Englishman to the core—can speak with hearty
good will or admiration of the Americans so long as
they cherish traditional feeling against the Old Country.
It is a mean tradition, unworthy of a great people.
It is in fact the old Colonial servility turned upside
down. Nor does it gain in dignity by being as it now
is, in part at least, a homage to a foreign vote and in
part the inspiration of Protectionism seeking its own
ends. We must admit, on the other hand, that it
was naturally aggravated by the conduct and language
of the Jingo party, both in Great Britain and here, at
the time of the Civil War. We must also admit that it
is partly explained by the political relations. Suppose
Scotland were a dependency of the United States and
an outpost of American democracy. Suppose the demo-
crats of Scotland were always playing up to the ambition
and the antipathies of their mother country by boasting
that they would prevent the extension of the power of
Great Britain over those islands and wrest a great cantle

from the realm of monarchical and aristocratic institutions. Suppose Presidential elections in Scotland were to be fought upon the line of antagonism to the neighbouring kingdom, with violent ebullitions of anti-British feeling. Is it not likely that there would be a good deal of anti-American feeling in Great Britain? After all, in the hearts of all the better Americans the sentiment is dying, and its death will be hastened by the International Copyright law, because hitherto the unfair competition to which American writers were exposed with pirated English works has helped to embitter them against England. Still no Englishman who reads what American journals and authors say of his country will be inclined to do the Americans more than justice. But to refuse to do them justice would be injustice to ourselves; we 'should thereby commit ourselves to a course of policy false and suicidal as well as unkind. Those who fling about the charges of pessimism perhaps do not attach much meaning to the word, otherwise we might ask them whether anything can be more pessimistic than the assumption that one moiety of this English-speaking continent is always to be on bad terms with the other. Does not the refusal to believe in friendship with the rest of our race deserve the gloomy epithet as much as the refusal to believe that the country can be on the high road to prosperity under a system of monopoly and corruption?

Twenty-seven years have passed since I first made acquaintance with the United States. It was at the time
of the Civil War. I came out to bear to the North the
sympathies of friends in England opposed to slavery,
to see for them how the struggle was really going, and
on my own account to witness a great political spectacle.
I have always thought that the two most trying tests of
national character are plague and civil war. The first
thing that struck me was the absence of anything to tell
one that a civil war was raging. It is true that this
was an unusual case, the nation having split into halves
and the fighting being confined to the Southern region.
Still the national peril was extreme, the excitement was
intense, and it was remarkable that social, industrial and
commercial life should be going on so calmly as it was.
Civil law prevailed, personal liberty was enjoyed, the
press was free, and criticized without reserve the acts of
the government and the conduct of the war. At the
Presidential election which I witnessed there was no in-
terference with the liberty of speech or of the suffrage.
Fiercely as the passions of the majority were roused, the
minority was allowed to hold its public meetings, to
celebrate its torchlight processions, to hang out its ban-
ners across the public way. On the election day order
was hardly any where disturbed. The next thing that
struck me was the union of classes. The same patriotism seemed to pervade them all. We had been told that
the rich, being politically ostracised, were disaffected to

the Republic; but this many of them at all events by
their devotion to her cause, their self-sacrifice, and the
cheerfulness with which they bore the public burdens,
belied. The third thing that struck me was the unity of
the different States. We had been led to believe in
England that the East was dragging on the unwilling
West; but I was soon able to report that this was utterly
untrue and that even if the East were willing to stop
the West would not. In the fourth place, I was agree-
ably surprised by the absence, in word and deed, of the
inhumanity by which civil war is generally stained. I
saw the prison camps and satisfied myself that the in-
mates were suffering no hardship not inseparable from
their condition of prisoners of war. I saw a prison hospital in which the patients were as carefully treated as
they could be in any hospital, and the table was spread
for the convalescents on Thanksgiving Day with all the
good things of the season. This was when the North
was ringing with the reports of the cruel treatment of
its soldiers in Confederate prison camps. Scarcely ever
did I hear even an utterance of truculent sentiment
against the South. The people generally said that they
were fighting to assert the law, and that if the South
would submit to the law they did not wish to do it any
further harm. No vengeance was taken by the victors;
not a drop of blood was shed on the political scaffold; no
penalties were inflicted beyond civil disabilities, and even
these were speedily removed. Europe, looking to the

history of previous civil wars, believed that an overthrow of the Constitution by the army and a military usurpation would be the end. The result was a glorious contradiction of that belief. Great powers were necessarily thrown into the hands of President Lincoln, but he never betrayed the slightest inclination to abuse or even to enlarge them; and when a general, flushed with victory, allowed himself to be betrayed into an encroachment on the authority of the civil government, his soldiers, though they adored him, showed that they would not follow him beyond the line of his duty. The Constitution came through the Civil War unchanged, or changed only in the direction of liberty. Respect for law, which is the sheet-anchor of republics, could in that republic scarcely be wanting.

Political evils and dangers in the United States, of course there are. There is corruption in American politics. I do not believe now that anybody at Washington can be bought. But there is corruption in some State Legislatures. At Washington there is still the purchase of powerful votes, such as that of the protected manufactures or that of the Grand Army at the expense of the public policy and the interest of the taxpayer. But is corruption, or the purchase of the votes of protected manufacturers and other interests by sinister concessions, confined to the United States? It is as needless as it would be nauseous to dwell on the revelations which are filling all Canadians with grief and shame. When was a President of the United States who sought re-election, found assembling the protected manufacturers in a Red Parlour and taking their contributions to his election fund ? When was it proved that an American Minister of State had been forming illicit relations with public contractors and taking money from them for political purposes, while he allowed them to defraud the State ? The Americans are not callous. A leading politician was driven from public life for an act of corruption which in some countries would be thought venial, and a bare suspicion of something of the kind cost a popular and powerful candidate his election to the Presidency. The elective system of government is everywhere on its trial. Nowhere has it yet been proved that the system can be carried on without party ; that party, when there is no great issue of principle, can be prevented from becoming faction ; or that a faction can be held together by any means but corruption. The same experiment is being made in the United States, in Canada, in the Parliamentary countries of Europe, and in Australia ; and everywhere in its present stage it wears the same doubtful aspect. Government for the people, we hope and trust, will never again perish from the earth : whether government by the people can endure, and in what form, is the great political problem of these days.

Somebody is very fond of throwing in my teeth something which I wrote about the evils and perils of Presi-

dential elections. I have not a word to retract. Presidential elections, as now conducted, are an excrescence
on the American Constitution, the framers of which intended the election to be made, not by popular suffrage
with a furious conflict between parties, but by a college
of select citizens in a tranquil and deliberate way;
though it is strange that men so sagacious should not
have foreseen what the practical working of their machinery would be. These contests, which evoke almost
the passions of a civil war, will have to be discontinued
or mitigated if the Republic is to endure: perhaps if
Canada ever joins the Union the opportunity of constitutional revision may be embraced, and some improvement in Presidential elections may be made. But those
who bid us compare with the turbulence of a Presidential election in the United States the tranquil appointment of a Governor-General of Canada are looking for
the point of comparison in the wrong place. The Governor-General does not answer to the President. When
there is a crisis in American politics the President is
always at Washington. When there is a crisis in Canadian politics the Governor-General goes fishing. What
answers to the Presidency here is the Premiership, and
the counterpart of a Presidential election is not the
appointment of a Governor-General but the General Election, at which the question who shall be Premier is virtually decided. We have just had one of these general
elections, and I would ask, looking back on that election,

on the manner in which and the time at which it was
brought on, the pretence put forth for the Dissolution,
the real motive for it which now appears, the part which
the Governor-General was made passively to play in
palming a falsehood upon the nation, the issue on which
the battle was fought, and which involved the treatment
of half the citizens not as dissidents but as traitors, the
means by which the Government gained its victory, including the bribery of provinces and constituencies with
promises of public outlay—looking back on all this, I
say, are you prepared to say that there is much difference to our advantage between a Presidential election in
the United States and a general election in this country? When was the American nation insulted by bringing one of its ambassadors from Europe to take the lead in
a party conflict and ply the engine of party corruption?
When did public men of the highest standing in the
United States, to fix an infamous charge on their opponents, make use of documents filched from printing
offices or of stolen letters? If to the men who do such
things public monuments are raised, honour will desire
to rest in an unnoted grave. Observe, too, that the Imperial government, from the political and moral tutelage
of which such benefits are supposed to be derived, ap-
proved, in the person of Lord Salisbury, the fraud prac-
tised on the nation and cabled its congratulations on the
victory of corruption. Nay, it was from England, as
there seems reason to believe, that the word came com-

manding the managers of a Canadian railway built with
public money to aid a party government in trampling on.
public right.

The excesses of party spirit among our neighbours, it
must be granted, are often deplorable, and most fatal to
the commonweal. But are they less deplorable or less
fatal to the commonweal here ? Are not we in Canada
always flying at each other's throats for mere political
Shibboleths and sacrificing to an empty name our country's manifest interest and our own ? Does not faction
among us, as well as among our neighbours and kinsmen,
condone dishonesty, wink at public theft, prefer the
rogue who wears its own colours to the honest man who
wears the colours of the other party or none at all ? In
which constituency of this Dominion would simple up-
rightness, ability and patriotism, wearing the colour of
neither faction, receive a dozen votes ? Is the evil machinery of party, with its bosses, its wirepullers, confined to the American Commonwealth ? Is it in the
American Commonwealth alone that the service of party
gives birth to a swarm of place-hunters, seeking to feed
upon the public instead of making their bread by honest
trades ? Everything with us is on a smaller scale, but
otherwise are not all things much the same ? Have we
not the same political difficulties to struggle against and
the same good and steadfast hope of surmounting them
in the end ?

We all know what there is to be said, and what patriotic Americans say, against the American Press, especially against the party journals; and evils in this quarter are most serious, because the power of the Press being
so great as it is, whatever poisons journalism poisons the
mind and heart of a nation. But let me ask you, can you
name any two organs in the United States, or anywhere
else, which have done more to disgrace journalism, to de-
prave the public taste, to degrade political discussion into
a slanderous brawl, and to fill the community with mean
and malignant passions, than the two successive personal
organs of a Tory Prime Minister of Canada?

We are told to consider the massacre at New Orleans,
and then say whether we will have anything to do with
people among whom such atrocities can take place. The
murder club which, by assassinating a city officer, created
the public panic and provoked the massacre, was not
American or Republican. It was Italian, the offspring
of a country which, for many centuries, had been under
the government of the despot and the priest. Louisiana
is not like New England. It is an old Slave State, and
slavery has everywhere left its traces, in a disregard
for the sanctity of human life. This is the account
of the lynchings of negroes, which still disgrace
the South, and probably of the long list of unpunished
murders in Kentucky. But who are they among us that
point the finger of reprobation at the violence which

slavery bred? They are the very men who, when the
mortal struggle between Freedom and Slavery was going
on, were the enthusiastic friends and backers of the
Slave Power.

Municipal maladministration, waste and malversation,
again, are too prevalent in the United States. But are
they less prevalent under the same system of municipal
government elsewhere? Is not the elective system of
government for cities, as well as for nations everywhere,
still on its trial? Does anybody, in any country, feel yet
assured of its success? Tammany, no doubt, is of all
municipal scandals the greatest : but Tammany is a
foreign gang.

The foreign element in the United States is another
bugbear often held up by those who would scare us
away from the connection. The foreign element is un-
questionably a source of danger, and the Americans themselves, by the legislative restrictions which they are im-
posing on immigration, show that they are alive to the
fact. But is the influence of the foreign element on the
councils of the American commonwealth more alien in
its character or more sinister than the influence of the
French element on ours?

Nor does anybody deny that there are social as well
as political evils and dangers in the United States. The
gravest of them perhaps are those which threaten the

family through the increasing frequency of divorce. But this disturbance, like the unsettlement of the relations between the sexes generally, is the malady of all countries, though at present in different degrees. Nor is the divorce law of Illinois and Indiana the divorce law of the whole Union. The tendency of American legislatures of late, I believe, has been rather against increased facility of divorce. At any rate we may maintain friendly relations and trade with our neighbours without adopting their divorce laws, or the theories which some of them may have embraced about the character and the proper functions of woman.

So it is with the industrial and economical disturbances ; in the lesser country they are on a smaller scale, but in kind they are common to the whole continent and to Europe and Australia as well. We have had our difficulties with the Knights of Labour and have seen labour disturbances in our streets. If we have not Trusts, we have Combines, organs, like the Trusts, of a spirit of grasping monopoly which seeks to engross the profits of trade regardless of the public weal. Nor is it easy to see how, without a far stronger government than our present system can furnish, the community is to be protected in either case.

The vulgar luxury and all the other evils which attend overgrown fortunes are of course at their height and most repulsive where the country being the richest, fortunes are most overgrown. No shoddy perhaps is so gorgeous as that of New York. But has New York a monopoly of shoddy? Does not every rich city in a commercial country produce wealth unrefined by culture, unennobled by duty, which solicits admiration by its magnificence and provokes the smile of contempt. We hope that this will everywhere be worked off by civilization in time. Nowhere has it been worked off yet.

Under the policy which at present prevails, we are constantly sending into the United States the flower of Canadian youth. Do these men become base and hateful when they cross the line? The two sections of English-speaking people are in a state of social fusion: that is the fact; and with fusion assimilation must come. Some men seem to fancy that they can make themselves English gentlemen by parading contempt for Yankees. Let them indulge the fancy and be happy. But the truth is that if you were taken with your eyes bandaged from Canadian to American society, you would hardly be conscious of the change. One cannot help thinking, when some of our Jingoes are reviling the Yankee, that if we are to quarrel with the United States for the difference between them and the Yankee, it will be the smallest bone of contention that ever set two nations by the ears.

All these imaginary or conventional antipathies, whether political or social, are apt to betray their unreality as soon as the touchstone of interest is applied. How many Jingoes are there who would refuse a good berth on the other side of the line? Some of the most violent abuse of the Continental Policy and party here comes from Canadian Jingoes settled in the United States. Yet these patriots have not scrupled where their own interest was concerned to embrace a policy eminently Continental.

Our book-stores and libraries are full of American literature. Our magazine literature is chiefly American. Not only our intellectual tastes but our moral and social character will be in some danger if we are always imbibing the effusions of depravity and baseness.

It is not likely, gentlemen, that I shall ever again address you or any other audience on the subject of Canadian politics. A political student when to the best of his power he has laid a question in all its bearings before the community has done all that it pertains to him to do and must leave the rest to the practical politician. Besides, the sand in my hour-glass is low, and before it quite runs out, there are a few things gathered during a student's life which I should like, if I can, to put in shape. I see it is said again that nothing which I write can take hold because I have never shared the national aspirations. There are plenty of other reasons why what I write should not take hold, but as I showed in my first lecture, it is not true that I have never shared the national aspirations. Aspirations for perpetual dependence and colonial peerages with which some bosoms seem to swell, I have not shared; national aspirations I have. If you had time to waste in looking back to the old files of the two great party organs of former days, you will find frequent amenities bestowed on me for sympathizing with what was then called "Canada First." I was singled out for attack, because to attack a new-comer was much safer than to attack some who, though much more prominent, had followings and connections here. As I have said before, I never belonged to the Canada First Association. Membership of a political organization would hardly have become one who had only just settled in this country. But I did very heartily sympathize with the desire of making Canada a nation, which was the vision of my lamented friend Mr. W. A. Foster and the generous youth of Canada at that day; and I gave the movement such assistance as I could with my pen. The movement, however, at that time failed : its flag was suddenly allowed to fall : the star which had risen in the East and which it had followed ceased to shine. Then I, like others, had to review the situation. A community could not become a nation or acquire the national attributes of force, spirit and dignity without independence. So far the hearts of Canada First had pointed true. But otherwise, was their vision capable of realization ? There can be no use in pursuing what is not practicable, however noble or

however fondly cherished our idea may be. Was there
any real hope of blending into a nation these Provinces
geographically so disjointed, and so destitute of any
bond of commercial union among themselves, while each
of them separately is so powerfully attracted by commercial interest to the great English-speaking community on
the South of it ? Was there any real hope of fusing
French with British Canada, or if they could not be
fused, of bringing about a national union between them?
These questions cannot be settled by our wishes or decided on horseback. I found myself compelled to answer
both of them in the negative. From that time it has
been my conviction that the end would be a return
of the whole English-speaking race upon this continent
to the union which the American Revolution broke,
that to prepare for this was the task of Canadian
statesmanship, and that to spend millions upon millions
in vainly struggling to avert it was to waste the earnings
of our people. All that has happened since has confirm-
ed me in this belief. The difficulty of holding the Confederation together and keeping it apart from the rest of
the continent, otherwise than by corruption, has seemed
to me half to excuse the system of Sir John Macdonald,
calamitous as the consequences of that system have been
not only to the finances and the material prosperity, but
to the character of our people. Nor, noble as may be
the dream of a separate nationality, does it appear to me
that our lot will be mean if we are destined to play our

full part in the development of civilization on this broad
continent, which we hope is to be the scene of an im-
proved and a happier humanity. Let us have hearts for
the romantic and heroic past; let us have hearts also for
the grand realities of life. There would surely be nothing shameful in a compact like that by which Scotland
united her illustrious fortunes with the illustrious fortunes of her partner in Great Britain. There can never
be a reason why we should break with our history or
discard anything that is valuable in our traditions and, it
may be, in our special character as colonists of Britain
who have preserved the tie. In a vast Federal Union
there will always be many mansions for character, and
Ontario as well as Massachusetts or Virginia may keep
her own. To help in making Ontario keep her own
character in the literary sphere and in building up her
intellectual life, has been my Jingoism, Jingoism of a
very mild type it must be owned. Of course I understand and respect: not only do I understand and respect,
but I heartily share reluctance to leave the side of the
mother country. But we should not in any real sense
leave her side by mere political separation : probably we
should draw back to her side this English-speaking continent, which it is the tendency of political complications
to estrange. To be run politically by a backstairs
clique in Downing Street, or by operators in the London
railway share market, is not to be at the side of the
mother country. England sways us far more by her

books than through her Governors. The interest of the British people is one with that of the Canadian people, as the British people begin to see. Their consent to any changes is, by me at least, always supposed. Of the Imperial Federationists I never said a harsh word. I sincerely respect their aspirations. But there are at least three parties among them, that of the Parliamentary Federationists, that of the War Federationists, and that of the Commercial Federationists, each of them at variance with the others, while, after twenty years of eloquent exposition not one of them has yet ventured on any practical step for the fulfilment of its idea. Let them put the question to one legislature, Imperial or Colonial, and let us see what the answer will be.

I know too well that these opinions are distasteful to many. They are distasteful perhaps to many of my present audience whose thoughts and efforts point a different way. That they are gross and unsentimental, because union with our Continent would bring an increase of the material prosperity to our people, I cannot admit. Political and military sentiment are excellent in their way and within reasonable limits, but there is a sentiment also attached to material wellbeing; it is the sentiment which waits on well-rewarded industry and has its seat in happy and smiling homes. What is the object of all our political arrangements if it is not to give us happiness in our homes? Empire which is not happiness, even though it may be world-wide, is not great-

ness. However, be my opinions right or wrong, my con-
victions have been deliberately formed and are sincere.
A political student is neither bound nor excused by the
exigencies of statecraft. He can serve the community
only by speaking, to the best of his power, the truth
and the whole truth.

While I, gentlemen, am leaving the scene, you are entering on public life. I would with my parting words
conjure you at all events to look facts steadily in the
face, and make up your mind one way or the other.
You can afford to drift no longer. Whether your highest aim be to live and die British subjects, or to live and
die members of an Imperial Federation, or to live and
die Canadian freemen and citizens of this Continent,
firmly embrace the policy which will lead you to that
mark. Your people will not be content always to have
poorer chances and to be worse off than their neighbours.
They are beginning to signify this in more ways than,
one, above all by the melancholy token of the Exodus.
Both Lord Durham and Lord Elgin told you that it
would be so. Both of them said that commercial reciprocity and equality with the United States were indispensable. Blindness to the future often styles itself
practical wisdom, but the title is usurped and in no case
more usurped than in ours. The Census tells us, with a.
clear, sad voice, what, if we take no thought for the.
future, the future is likely to be. For the few who,
profit by the system there may be large fortunes and

baronial mansions in England, where they will win
titles and social consequence by making Canada move,
or pretending to make her move, in conformity with the
interest of an aristocratic party in Great Britain.
For the people at large there will be the inevitable fate
of a country kept by artificial separation and restriction
below the level of its Continent in commercial prosperity and in the rewards held out to industry. There will
be a perpetual exodus of the flower of our population to
the more prosperous and hopeful field ; Manitoba and the
North-West, excluded from the commercial pale of their
continent and barred against the inflow of its migratory population, will continue to lag in the Census and in
the records of material prosperity behind the neighbouring States. This loss of our active spirits will be at-
tended with a political deadness, such as we already
see accompanying commercial depression in those mari-
time provinces with which under an evil star Ontario
has become politically bound up. With the neediness of
the constituencies venality and servility will increase,
and the grip of corruption will thus become stronger
than ever. So things may go on for a long time, the
very impoverishment and depletion which the system
causes being the evil securities for its continuance. But
at last the inevitable will come. It will come, and
when it does come it will not be that equal and honourable Union of which alone a patriotic Canadian can bear
to think ; it will be Annexation indeed.

www.ingramcontent.com/pod-product-compliance
Lightning Source LLC
Chambersburg PA
CBHW031438270326
41930CB00007B/771